GW00707651

PARTICIPATION
Spice it up!

Practical tools for
engaging children and
young people in planning
and consultations

Save the Children is the UK's leading international children's charity. Working in more than 70 countries, we run emergency relief alongside long-term development and prevention work to help children, their families and communities to be self-sufficient.

Drawing on this practical experience, Save the Children also seeks to influence policy and practice to achieve lasting benefits for children within their communities. In all its work, Save the Children endeavours to make children's rights a reality.

Published by The Save the Children Fund 2002.

Achub y Plant/Save the Children
2nd Floor, Phoenix House
8 Cathedral Road
CARDIFF CF11 9LJ

REGISTERED CHARITY NO. 213890

Dynamix Ltd
Unit 4D, Cwm Road
Hafod, Swansea
SA1 2AY
Tel: 01792 466231
Email: info@dynamix.ltd.uk
Web: www.dynamix.ltd.uk

ISBN 1 84187 062 5

All rights reserved. This publication is copyright, but may be reproduced by any method without fee or prior permission for teaching purposes, but not for resale. For copying in other circumstances, prior written permission must be obtained from the publisher and a fee may be payable.

A CIP record for this book is available from the British Library.

In compiling this publication every effort has been made to ensure the accuracy of the information. However, Dynamix and Save the Children do not assume and hereby disclaim any liability to any party for loss or damage caused by errors or omissions in this publication whether such errors or omissions result from negligence, accident or other cause.

Cartoons by Les Evans
Edited by Anita Holford anita@writing-services.co.uk
Design and print by Carrick
Tel: 01443 843 520 www.carrickdesignprint.co.uk

Save the Children

At a time when throughout the UK, there is unprecedented interest from policy makers and practitioners alike in the 'how' of involving children and young people, the Wales Programme of Save the Children (Achub y Plant) is pleased to have been able to commission Dynamix to produce this publication.

To really change things for children, and to ensure that their right to participate becomes an everyday reality in schools and communities, children and young people's participation has to become a mainstream activity throughout our public services. Save the Children shares with Dynamix a strong commitment to spreading the knowledge, experience, techniques, methods, values and philosophy of their creative approach amongst all those working with and for children and young people. We can all support children and young people's participation and this publication tells us how!

About the Authors

This book was written on behalf of Dynamix by Carol Shephard, co-director of Dynamix since 1996 and Phil Treseder, Development Officer for Save the Children Wales and freelance consultant. Dynamix is a creative training co-operative based in Swansea, Wales which is committed to 'Serious Fun'. Since 1988 we have sought to challenge the conventions around consultation and have gathered and devised a wide range of activities and methods to ensure we can explore even very serious issues in a fun way. Serious Fun is an approach which runs throughout our work, and we hope through this book, to encourage others to adopt a seriously fun approach to participation and inclusion.

Acknowledgments

Dynamix would like to thank the Wales Programme of Save the Children (Achub y Plant) for commissioning this book, and also the steering team of Mike Lewis, Nigel Clarke, Anne Crowley, Darren Bird, Carol Shephard, Phill Burton, Peter Duncan and Phil Treseder. Also thanks to Ali Morrison for all the typing and all the Dynamix workers who have contributed to the development of the activities and this book. Thanks also to everybody we have worked and played with. A final thank you to Issy Cole-Hamilton for coming up with the idea of the publication several years ago and nagging us until we finally got around to it.

FOREWORD

I welcome this guide to participative working with young people. Here in Wales we have embarked on a mission to transform the way in which we provide services for all our young citizens. At the heart of that transformation is the commitment to find out what young people think and feel, and to involve them directly and meaningfully in the decisions that affect them.
To do this we need to find new ways for adults and young people to interact, new approaches that work for both. Many adults are well disposed to such ideas, but do not feel they have the skills to get on. Many young people are uninspired by conventional adult approaches.
With this guide, Dynamix is making a significant contribution to enable us to progress. It offers a clear statement of the values on which its work is based, and practical methods that I have seen working in action.

Peter Clarke
Children's Commissioner for Wales

Over the past couple of years, I have used the methods in this book in the work I have done for The Children and Young People's Assembly, an organisation which gives children and young people a voice at a national level. We have used these methods in the conferences and consultations we have planned and facilitated. They always get the results in a fun way that does not put people on the spot: everybody gets the opportunity to add their ideas and opinions. Dynamix has also given us lots of ideas for less serious games so when people are tired and ideas have run out we are able to get up, get moving and have some fun. Being able to have a say in what affects you is the best way to get a service which works, and the methods that Dynamix has passed on to us have been a great way of getting those voices heard.

Becky Lythgoe,
Young person and development worker,
Children and Young People's Assembly, Wales.

CONTENTS

PART 1

SETTING THE SCENE

PART 2

VALUES, PRACTICE AND ISSUES

PART 3

THE TOOLKIT

PART 4

COOKING WITH DYNAMIX: THINGS TO HELP YOU

PART 5

MORE ABOUT DYNAMIX

PART 1
SETTING THE SCENE

INTRODUCING THIS BOOK

Now, I bet you're curious to know why they have written this book and whether it's for you!

WHY ARE WE WRITING THIS BOOK?

Many people have asked us, "why don't you write a book?" and we now feel the time has come to share the work we do and methods we use with a wider audience. In this first section we aim to give you an insight into our philosophy and motivation. We want you to understand why we do what we do, and we want to give you some practical tools - games and activities, ideas for how to use them, and hints on planning and running sessions. However, right from the start we want to share our anarchy with you and stress that all these ideas are there to be used, adapted and passed on, just as we have used, adapted and passed on our own and other people's ideas in the lead up to this book.

WHO ARE 'WE'?

You'll already have read that this book has been written by one of the co-directors of Dyamix, a creative training co-operative based in Swansea, Wales. We didn't want to hold you up at this stage by telling you all about our work, but we'd love you to read more about it! So if you're interested, turn to Part 5 where you'll find out about who we are and what we do, including a few short case-studies.

WHO IS THE BOOK AIMED AT?

Participation – Spice it up! is for anyone who wishes to consult or involve children and young people in any setting. We are writing this book for people who want to create change and have the power to facilitate it. You don't have to be a qualified teacher or youth worker to use Dynamix methods, you just need the desire to implement change in a creative way. We have used our activities in educational, leisure, commercial, therapeutic and even social settings. We have used the methodology to facilitate team building, whole school policy making, consultations, fun days, curriculum development and play leader training. We have explored issues such as anti-bullying, the environment, life-long learning, promoting participation, raising self-esteem, behaviour and discipline and tackling problems of young people who feel excluded.

HOW TO USE THIS BOOK

Please read the philosophy bit. You only need to read it once if you want, but we really want you to understand the attitudes that underlie our ideas. The book is written in sections for you to dip into in whatever order you choose. We want to help you plan creatively, so there are some sample programmes to follow (or ignore!), details of further reading and resources, and check lists for each activity, to allow you to learn from our experience. The methodology section is laid out as clearly as possible, but please think about how you will use the methods and take time for preparation.

ABOUT THE TITLE – AND ABOUT SERIOUS FUN

Planning and consultations can be very scary, exclusive or worst of all... boring. The whole process can be dry or hidden beneath jargon and statistics, and those who consult may have few youth or play work skills. Planning and consultation is too important for us to thoughtlessly exclude the large groups in our world who would run away from questionnaires and other formality. So we want to show how you can bring questions to creative life - all it takes is a bit of imagination, a desire for serious fun and a touch of spice. By that we mean make it relevant, interesting, participative and fun.

AGE RANGE

The methods in this book have been used with children and young people from the ages of 18 months to 25 years and beyond. The methodology sections do not provide a suggested age range as everything can be adapted with a little imagination – look out for the adaptation sections. It is important to remember not to underestimate the ability of all children and young people to participate – the fact is, they can. Don't let your preconceptions about their age, ability or reputation stop you from consulting any child. If you feel that your colleagues need a little creativity, you can also use the methods on adults. We do – they enjoy the change from the usual stuffy meeting or conference.

DEFINITIONS AND BACKGROUND

Participation: definitions of terms

For the purpose of this book we need to first
clarify some of the common words around
participation, including:

Involvement
Consultation
Participation
Empowerment
Citizenship

They don't like jargon but they do use it a bit — at least they are trying to explain it here.

Involvement in decision-making can start with
tokenism and end in control. Many people may be
aware of the ladder of participation (Hart, 1992). The alternative
model below highlights the degrees of involvement in decision-making
in a circular layout. The non-hierarchical model recognises the fact
that in certain areas – for example, in schools – involvement will never
result in control.

Consulted & informed
The project is designed
and run by adults but
children are consulted.
They have a full
understanding of the
process & their opinions
are taken seriously

Assigned but informed
Adults decide on the
project & children
volunteer for it. The
children understand the
project, they know who
decided to involve them
& why. Adults respect
young people's views

**Adult-initiated, shared
decisions with children**
Adults have the initial
idea but young people
are involved in every
step of planning &
implementation. Not
only are their views
considered but children
are also involved in
making the decisions

**Child-initiated, shared decisions
with adults**
Children have the ideas, set up
projects & come to adults for advice,
discussion & support. The adults
do not direct but offer their
expertise for young people to consider

**Degrees
of
Involvement**

Child-initiated & directed
Young people have the initial idea
& decide how the project is to be
carried out. Adults are available
but do not take charge

From: Empowering children & young people training manual: promoting involvement in
decision making (Save the Children). Phil Treseder, 1997.

Consultation is a process that has been thought through in terms of aims, methodology, how views will be taken on board and how they will be fed back to the group. Anything less is tokenism.

Participation and Empowerment – the terms are often used interchangeably in this context, but are not the same thing. Participation is the process of involving children and young people in decision-making. The outcome of any successful participation process will be empowered children and young people.

Citizenship – Save the Children define the concept as follows: 'Citizenship implies that children develop values, skills and understanding which enable them to become responsible adults – but it is not just about becoming responsible adults. It recognises that children now have civil and political rights to participate and represent themselves in political, educational, social and economic processes and systems. It is also about their entitlement to be empowered to participate in society effectively as active, informal, critical and responsive citizens.'

Any informed participation of children and young people will contribute towards their development as citizens.

The right to participate

'States Parties shall assure to the child who is capable of forming his or her own views the right to express those views freely in all matters affecting the child, the views of the child being given due weight in accordance with age and maturity of the child.

For this purpose the child shall in particular be provided the opportunity to be heard in any judicial and administrative proceedings affecting the child, either directly or through a representative or an appropriate body, in a manner consistent with the procedural rules of national law.'

Article 12
United Nations Convention on the Rights of the Child

In December 1991 the UK Government ratified the United Nations Convention on the Rights of the Child (UNCRC) and by doing so committed itself under international law to all the associated articles and principles. One of the most significant is Article 12, but to this day consultations with children and young people show that they still feel that adults do not listen to them or respect them. They have low status, little power and almost no control over their own lives within the family, school, public services or in relation to politicians and policy makers.

However, change is underway. In Wales, greater recognition has been given to the voices of children and young people, particularly following the Waterhouse Report into abuse in care in North Wales. The enquiry showed that it should be fundamental for children and young people's voices to be heard – and only when this is a part of everyday life can we be sure that children and young people are being properly protected. By following Article 12, we can be sure that young people are developing the skills they need in order to function fully as adult citizens.

Children Act 1989 and related policy initiatives

The recognition of the right for children and young people to participate in decision-making - along with a number of high profile scandals around care in the 1970s through to the 1990s – led to improvements being included in the Children Act (1989) and the subsequent development of Children's Rights and Advocacy services.

This in turn has helped to promote participation to wider statutory and voluntary services. In recent years, policymakers and politicians have also developed the level and profile of user involvement through policy initiatives such as Best Value, and the establishment of the Children and Young People's Unit at the Department for Education and Skills which promotes their participation in Government.

Policy initiatives from national government are also beginning to impact on local authorities and other local services. In Wales, consultation on the subject of extending children and young people's entitlements (the equivalent of the 'Connexions' scheme in England), and the publication of 'Children and Young people – a Framework for Partnership', clearly indicates that the National Assembly for Wales will expect local partnerships to include children and young people, and funding for mechanisms such as youth forums is currently being allocated to local authorities.

Together, all of these developments have meant that children and young people are now able to claim their human rights. This doesn't involve a straight exchange of power, but a negotiation, and a valuing of a child as a person in their own right, not simply an adjunct to their parents. The aim is to make children and young people visible in social policy, and to be clear that they have their own needs and rights – and participatory processes will help this.

> If you are completely new to involving children and young people in decision making, you can read more about all these issues in the titles listed in 'Reading and Resources', page 137.

Where do we go from here?

Despite all this, children and young people's contributions to the development of policies and services are far too often one-off and ad-hoc. Often their views and experiences are seen as irrelevant – but in fact, they are just the opposite. Only a child or young person can tell you why s/he plays truant from school or runs away from a care placement. Only children and young people can tell you what provision they and their peers need in a particular locality. The real lack of knowledge and experience lies with those of us who fail to draw out, listen to and act upon the knowledge and experience of children and young people. The challenge is to make participation a reality for all children and young people so that they are empowered to make a contribution to decisions that affect them as individuals and as a group, at a local and national level.

PART 2
VALUES, PRACTICE AND ISSUES TO CONSIDER

Dynamix have got quite excited about why their methodologies work and how people learn best

SECTION 1

Dynamix — Philosophy and Values

Underpinning all our work is a firm set of values based around the ideas of co-operation, participation, inclusion and empowerment. By this we mean:

- getting people working together to solve problems;
- providing activities where everyone has space to join in or have their say;
- adapting, improvising and listening to people's ideas so that everyone feels included;
- working with respect to build people's self esteem so that they feel confident to participate in our sessions and beyond.

These values, combined with a commitment to serious fun – taking our fun seriously and tackling serious issues in a fun way – have led us into areas of work broader than we could ever have imagined. If you want to know more, turn to Part Five: About Dynamix.

The methods in this book are all tried and tested and are central to the work we do. We have known for a long time that these methods work, and that our values were one of the keys to their success, but only after being established for nine years did we stop to reflect why this should be. The following 'onion' diagram was presented to us by Paul Ginnis, a respected authority on learning theory, as a way to make sense of what we instinctively knew.

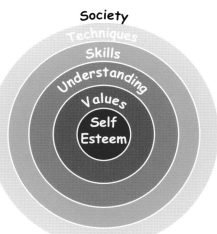

Society
Techniques
Skills
Understanding
Values
Self Esteem

Inside a good trainer

The 'onion' diagram (on the right) could equally be called 'Inside a Good Facilitator, Youth Worker, Educator, Teacher...'. In the centre of the onion is your own self-esteem. If you feel positive about yourself, your abilities and your value in your organisation or work then this will deeply impact on your effectiveness as a trainer. The next ring of the onion is values – having a strong set of values that influences your work will enable you to work consistently in different settings. If these values are shared within your organisation or at least amongst your colleagues – even better!

The next layer – understanding - is the one which we found we were lacking. As trainers for Dynamix we had a clear and firmly held set of values and a very supportive environment in which to build and maintain our self-esteem. We had strong skills in facilitation – such as listening and communication – and we were using the techniques described in this book very successfully. What we had not considered was the reason why all these elements made for successful training and work with young people. A lot of our understanding came from learning about brain theory and teaching and learning styles (if you want to look more deeply into this, see the Further Reading and Resources list). However, we came to understand that participative methodology, combined with values centred on co-operation, inclusion and empowerment make for a good learning environment too. The following is just one example of research which backs up this thinking.

How children and young people learn

Participative methods of learning can have significant impact on children and young people. Researchers in the United States showed that only 30% of students remember even 75% of what they hear in an average lesson. Children and young people learn through:

- A wide variety of every day experiences inside and outside schools
- By knowing what they aim to achieve and why
- By researching, rather than being told everything they need to know
- By discussing and co-operating with peers in tackling tasks
- By contact with adults
- By evaluating outcomes and planning further work
- By having opportunities to take responsibility for planning and organising various aspects of work
- Through allowing experimentation, reflection and extension
- Through practice and repetition
- By 'doing'
- By making choices
- By reflecting on what they are doing
- By explaining what they are doing to others
- By exploring and investigating
- By building on previous knowledge and experience
- By achieving success

From: Teaching & Learning Styles – Staff Development Pack – Oldham TVEI 1996.

SECTION 2

Issues to Consider

They also want you to have a think about why you're doing what you're doing...

If you're new to working with children and young people, you'll find further reading on issues around involvement in decision making (e.g. Empowering Children and Young People: Training Manual, Treseder, 1997) and on legal issues (e.g. Working with Young People – Legal Responsibility and Liability 5th Edition, Children's Legal Centre) in Part 4, beginning on page 137, Further Reading and Resources.

For readers who feel it is time to dip their toes in the water, a word of warning – **PREPARATION!**

We hope you will find the methodology in Part Three (beginning on Page 21) helpful, but it will be of much more use if you first consider a number of other factors. This section will help, before you move on to the next stage.

Involving children and young people in decision-making

Let's face the facts - there is a down side to this after all. Start down this particular road and they will expect to have a voice and will expect you to listen. What's more, they will expect you to continue the process in the future. They will even expect something to happen as a result.

Why do you want to involve children and young people?

It is essential that you have the support of your colleagues and managers before you attempt to involve children and young people.

People who will be involved or affected need to be committed to the rights of children and young people or to recognise that the benefits will outweigh any extra resources and time that will be needed. Embarking on the road towards empowerment is likely to end in failure and frustration if those around you are not supportive and block your good intentions. If the outcome of your discussions is that you do not wish to involve children and young people or that the necessary support is not available, then it may well be better to accept that situation rather than frustrating yourself and the children and young people. However, you should be honest, state your position and justify it to everyone involved.

What will the children and young people get out of it?

All too often the answer is, not a lot. For children and young people to sustain any interest they need to be getting something out of being involved. Part of that may well be the new skills and knowledge they will gain. But as with adults, many children and young people are looking to use their valuable spare time for something that will be interesting, fun and add to their social life, or because it represents something that they believe in. In general they are happy to be consulted and keen to become involved, but a balance is needed. Be careful not to exploit keen children and young people, for example involving them in a long consultation around play provision and in doing so, denying them time to play.

Are you prepared for the resource implications?

Participation is an ongoing process that will require commitment in terms of staff time and resources. If the process is to be successful then you'll need to consider:

- Extra costs – such as expenses for children and young people to attend meetings and other related conferences;

- Training – which may be needed so that real empowerment can be achieved, and ideally will be residential to encourage bonding and give something back to the participants;

- Staff time – including time for training, ongoing communication with the group, preparation for meetings (most of which are likely to be evenings or weekends) and general administration for the group;

- Resources – such as access to phones and word-processors to enable the children and young people to be able to carry out tasks themselves.

An extra word about resources

People are often concerned about the extra resources needed to allow meaningful involvement of children and young people. This can be easily justified if you consider the resources that can be wasted on facilities and services that don't meet the needs of a particular group.

In one such case, a rural community centre contacted their youth officer for advice on involving young people. The group of mainly elderly users were genuinely concerned about the lack of local provision in the area, which they felt was contributing to an increase in the level of crime and late night disturbances. As a result they raised £500 through various activities which they decided to spend on facilities that would attract young people into the centre. The group spent the money on sewing machines and other similar craft materials, believing that it would attract young women to the centre and young men would soon follow as a result. Good intentions, hard work - and £500 gone to waste.

Who should be involved?

All children and young people have the right to be involved in decision making. However, if you are a service provider with no specific group of young people with which to work directly, you'll need to consider who you should target. For example, a library service wishing to consult with children and young people about general improvements to the service might approach an established group such as a local youth forum who are used to being consulted and may have a wider range of experiences and geographical spread than, say, a particular school. However, a library serving a particular community might wish to focus its consultation on local schools and youth groups. Either way, you will also need to think about what commitment you require from the group. Established groups such as youth forums receive many requests for views and often have a full agenda. Local children may be prepared to attend a one-off event, but not so keen to join an advisory committee.

Once you've considered the above issues, you're ready to plan your consultation.

SECTION 3

Planning and Running a session

Thinking it through

Now that you have found out as much as you can about involving children and young people in your work, you need to decide what you're going to do in a consultation session. The starting point is the timetable – how much time do you have? You can make a list of everything you need to include (bearing in mind icebreakers, ground-rules and evaluation) then see if it will fit in with the time. You can use the menus of possible activities in Part 4 for inspiration. We often begin with the diagram below which uses a cooking analogy:

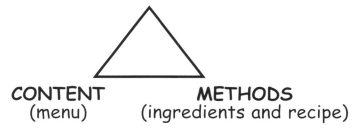

AIMS
(To make a good meal)

CONTENT
(menu)

METHODS
(ingredients and recipe)

Start by clarifying your aims then begin to fill in other parts of the triangle. What should the content of your session be? Are there certain methods you are keen to use or are particularly comfortable with? Begin to match content to methods bearing in mind your aims and, with a bit of luck, a programme will begin to form before your very eyes!

For example:

Swansea Youth Forum Consultation

AIMS
- Welcome & celebrate!
- To confirm what a forum is
- To take the forum forward
- To find ways to elect representatives

CONTENT
- Welcome, introductions
- Making it Work (ground-rules)
- Icebreaker/information gatherer
- What is a forum?
- What are its aims?
- Who should be there/representatives?
- How to get them there?
- How should it work?
- Feedback
- What next?
- End/Evaluation

METHOD
- Big group
- Ideas avalanche
- Reporters
- Hot seat from groups
- Post-its in groups
- Discussion Carousel
- Paper Carousel - the people identified
- Jigsaw
- How how how
- Targets

Risk assessment

Before you start, it's worth making your own risk assessment of the venue and the session. Get as much prior knowledge as possible but make your own final assessment – remember, other people may be more nervous or less innovative than you. Make safety a ground rule for everyone, whatever the content. Being aware of each other's physical and emotional safety is as important in a consultation as it is in a rock-climbing session, but be prepared to take calculated risks. If you are working in partnership you need to check that an appropriate risk for you is the same for the partner agency. Also check to see if they think that certain issues you want to discuss may be problematic.

For readers who are new to working with children or young people, please refer to 'Working with Young People - Legal responsibility and liability' from the Children's Legal Centre (see the Further Reading and Resources list). You will need to consider laws and guidances for vetting of staff, Children Act requirements for groups under the age of eight, and minibus legislation, to name but a few.

Running a Session

Preparation

Try to arrive with enough time to do some final preparation. Check the actual numbers of participants, have a look at the space you have to work in, check any safety issues in your surroundings.

Make sure you prepare some 'time fillers' or alternative activities in case you need them. Try to plan with others – it's often more fun that way and a different perspective can be very useful. Also, if you are using a new activity, try to have a practise beforehand.

Once you have identified your group, do a little more preparation – find out about their likes, dislikes and abilities and adapt your programme accordingly.

Making the most of the unexpected

When preparing for a workshop, try to think of all the things which could happen. This might help you to have some strategies at the ready, or it may make you panic if you have a vivid imagination!

If you can see the unexpected as an opportunity, a gift for you to improvise with, then you can relax and enjoy yourself, but don't forget if you're working as a team to communicate and co-ordinate with your colleagues!

Things to look out for

Make sure to respond to suggestions from the group – they can often see variations which might help you to be more inclusive. Also, it's more likely that they'll own a game or activity if they have adapted it themselves.

- Be aware of the energy and attention levels of your group and respond to them with activities to liven them up or calm them down as necessary. There is no point trying to have a serious discussion if everyone wants to run around, nor if they are half asleep.

- If people have stopped having fun, this is your biggest clue to do something different.

- You should always be aware of your group's physical and emotional safety. In your ground rules you will have established that safety is everyone's responsibility, but you will need to monitor it.

- We have talked about encouraging participant's suggestions and allowing them to take some control and create their own new games. However, not all suggestions will be appropriate: 'Kick the fat kid' is a not very new game that we once had to hastily stop.

- Finally, without becoming paranoid, you should be aware of how activities may be interpreted later by other people. If you are covering sensitive issues, think about the people who are peripheral to your group – parents, teachers and managers, who may need some clarification.

Advance preparation

No matter how much preparation you put in, there is always the possibility for something to go wrong. You learn from your mistakes and get on with it. The following tips and checklists should help you avoid some of the common pitfalls.

CHECK THE FOLLOWING IN ADVANCE:
CHILDREN AND YOUNG PEOPLE
- [ ] Aims of the session – are they clear?
- [ ] Age of the group
- [ ] Relevant background of the participants
- [ ] Any specific needs to be taken into account to aid inclusivity (bearing in mind that the greatest experts on any specific needs are the individuals themselves)
- [ ] Timing for the session and any breaks
- [ ] That you and the children/young people are not being used in any way that may be defined as tokenistic
- [ ] Who is responsible for what? (roles & responsibilities)
- [ ] That the children and young people are clear about what they are coming for
- [ ] Transport for children and young people
- [ ] Expenses are available in cash if required
- [ ] Are the refreshments suitable for children and young people?
- [ ] Can children and young people be involved in the facilitation?
- [ ] Are there enough breaks?
- [ ] Is the methodology age-appropriate?
- [ ] Is the time and day appropriate?
- [ ] Child protection procedures and confidentiality levels
- [ ] If appropriate, make sure the children and young people are aware of the level of confidentiality
- [ ] Any cultural barriers e.g. diet, customs

VENUE
- [ ] The space you have to work in
- [ ] Is the venue accessible?
- [ ] What equipment do you require?
- [ ] Is the venue young people friendly?
- [ ] The layout of the room
- [ ] Is the room comfortable, e.g. seats, temperature, fresh air

FOLLOW UP
- [ ] How will the information be fed back and to whom?
- [ ] If long term, is the initiative sustainable?
- [ ] How will the process be evaluated?
- [ ] Where will the information go and in what form?
- [ ] How will the young people be able to follow up what happens?

SECTION 4

Troubleshooting

This section provides tips and methods for keeping everybody involved. It is important to understand from the start that children and young people on the whole want to be involved in decision making. Yet at times events may conspire against you, depending on the group and the environment you are working in.

Making it Work
Troubleshooting before the trouble

A key element of every Dynamix programme is 'Making it Work'. This is a co-operative and positive way to establish some ground rules without the heaviness or challenge of "rules". We usually work on an **Ideas Avalanche** (see page 46) with the group to establish a deal which everyone agrees to stick to in order to make the session work. The responsibility for 'Making it Work' then rests with all of us, and it gives a reference point if problems arise later. As this happens early in a session it can be useful to have your own baseline suggestions ready in case the group are reluctant to speak early on. These might include listening to each other, respect, keeping it safe, having breaks. Try to let the group make the suggestions, as people tend to stick to deals which they have created and haven't been imposed on them. Stress that the rules are for everyone (including you!) and if people make suggestions that others are not prepared to keep, you will need to negotiate a compromise so that you all have a deal you are happy with.

If the group will be running over a period of time, keep the 'Making it Work' deals on flipchart, or laminate them. Put them on the wall each time the group meets and quickly remind everyone to check they are still happy to keep to them.

Relating to children and young people

There is no secret formula for working with children and young people, as the more experienced reader will know. Some of the key qualities are about being honest, treating people with respect, having a sense of humour, being open and approachable, being clear about professional boundaries, never patronising and always being accepting. You will also need to consider and take into account the needs, culture and attention span of the group.

It helps if you recognise that tangible results will take some time, that you will need to take criticism from time to time, learn from your mistakes, and be flexible in your approach. For those working with groups of children and young people who are socially excluded, the challenge is likely to be greater and results may take longer.

It is important to be yourself – if your normal dress for work is a suit and tie, then dress more casually if you can and tell everyone else to do the same. Don't go out and buy an expensive pair of trainers and a baseball cap – young people will see straight through you.

Now, things don't always go as smoothly as you might hope, so here are some ideas to help you reduce the chances of problems occuring......

Potential trouble points
1) By choice or not
A major influence on the success of the session is the reason for children and young people attending. Sessions should be attended out of choice, but on occasions there may be a different reason. We have run consultation sessions where young people have been deliberately misled to encourage them to attend. In a school situation, the reason may well be dodging double maths, rather than any real interest in the activity.

2) The issues
On occasions the issues being addressed may be particularly personal to the individuals in the group, and have the potential to upset participants – for example, discussing bullying in schools.

3) Previous experience
Some children and young people may have had negative experiences of being consulted or involved in planning and therefore have little or no confidence that this will be any different. Others may have never been asked their views and initially find the experience something of a culture shock.

4) Tension within the group
On occasions you may find that there are tensions between members of the group of which you are unaware.

The above trouble points are not easy to deal with, but if you prepare well, set up 'Making it Work', listen sensitively and use participative methods, their impact can be reduced.

Keeping everybody involved
Trust and teambuilding
Icebreakers and ground rule sessions are always needed and make a positive difference. Icebreakers can be found in Section Six. Even when the group know each other, do something just to warm them up.

Giving everybody an equal chance

As in any other group, you will get some shy types and some who engage in excessive communication! If you do feel there is a problem, here are some ideas to make the discussion more equal.

· Cotton bud debate   (see page 62)

· Talking stick   (see page 72)

· Discussion Carousel   (see page 50)

You can also use 'murmur time' by asking people to speak to the person next to them for a minute or two to get their ideas together. This also works well at the beginning of an Ideas Avalanche (see page 54) if you are greeted with silence. Another way to encourage enthusiastic participants to listen as well as share opinions is to insist they summarise what the person who spoke before them said, prior to making their own point.

Keeping everybody awake

Even when all is going well and the methodology is working, we all feel tired and start to get bored. Different groups and ages have varying concentration spans. It is always useful to have a 'wake up' exercise or two at the ready.

Research suggests that you are able to concentrate for the number of minutes that matches your age plus two minutes. This is a maximum for continued concentration and you peak at around 20 years – that's only 22 minutes!

The following games are useful for these purposes:

· Knots   (see page 110)

· Fruit Salad   (see page 112)

· Counting to Ten   (see page 110)

· On the Bank in the Pond   (see page 111)

And some activities to keep things lively and fun for everyone

Dynamix trainers often use parachute games with groups of all ages. These games are very co-operative and can be good for focusing, letting off steam, building self-esteem, trust and relaxation. Our parachute suppliers are listed in the Further Reading and Resources section (see page 138 - Play and Leisure) along with some books of parachute games.

Some of the games and methods described in this book involve physical contact. Always be aware of cultural and personal barriers to such activities and make it okay not to join in. Be prepared to adapt the activity to include everyone, or find a non-touching role for those who step back.

Dividing groups

Some problems may occur due to friends showing off to each other, or tensions within a group. For part of the time at least you may be able to split the participants into smaller groups. The easiest method is to number the participants to the number of groups you require - for example, 1 to 4. This is the best method for friends who need to be separated as inevitably they sit together. Other more creative options include:

- Jigsaw   (see page 28)

- Huggy Bear/Clumps   (see page 113)

- Alphabetical Archipelago   (see page 30)
  (once they are 'shuffled' into
  alphabetical order, put them in groups)

Use more interesting group names than just 'one, two, three, four' etc. Use fruits, pop bands, colours or, if you are doing issue based work, you could use something relevant to the subject e.g. names of drugs or contraceptives. Choose your theme to fit the group and get their attention!

Having fun with saboteurs

Sometimes someone, for whatever reason, wants to sabotage a session. As Article 19 of the United Nations Convention rules out violence, here are some alternatives!

Firstly, try to understand why they are behaving in a destructive way. Is the person bored? Could you engage them by giving them a role in the workshop? Do they have too much energy to participate in the current game? Could you use this energy? Do they feel powerless in the session? Could you give people choices so they feel they have some control over what they are doing?

Sometimes just recognising that someone's behaviour is intended to sabotage the session is enough to diffuse the situation and get them on 'your side'. Valuing their efforts as a new way of playing the game, or allowing their ideas to take you off on a tangent can also work to get them involved again. Maintaining a flexible attitude and being prepared to improvise with your group will help to overcome even the most challenging situations. In such difficult situations you can always return to the aims of the session or 'Making it Work' and check with the group that they feel on course.

First Aid

If things really do go horribly wrong here are some suggestions of ways to move forward:

- Recount what has gone before to allow time to gather your thoughts;

- Demonstrate a game or activity;

- Jump to something else and come back to that activity later;

- Don't be afraid to admit that something has gone wrong;

- Ask for help from fellow workers or participants themselves.

You may be surprised at the response to your plea for help. It is a powerful shift of status which often generates excellent solutions – solutions which you alone would probably never have thought of.

PART 3
THE TOOLKIT

SECTION 5

Introducing the Toolkit

If you have skipped the first part of the book and started here, we understand – we probably would too! But we really urge you to read the 'theory' sections because then you will understand where we are coming from. These methods all work. They work even better if you have a sound value base and theoretical understanding. After all, successful participation is not just about the activities you do.

You will see that the methods are set out with a title and a brief description of the activity. There is a key to tell you the approximate time needed for each activity and the number of participants with which it will work. Please note these are only guidelines – for each one we could have written 'depends on your group, depends on your subject, depends on the time of day' – not that this would help you much!

Next there is a basic description of how the activity works, followed by a section describing why we like it and a list of the resources needed. The second page of each method gives examples of when Dynamix has used the activity, links between that activity and others, and any developments or adaptations we know of. Finally there is a reference to the programmes where the methods have been used, and which are detailed in the Menu section at the back of the book (see also the index on page 141). So if you recognise the game, have a look at the second page – we might have found ways of using it that you had not thought of yet!

The activities are also split into four neat sections. These are by no means strict and although the activities all fit within their section, most can be used in a range of settings and at various points in a session. There's an index to the activities on page 140.

SECTION 6

Starting Activities

We have deliberately called this first section 'Starting Activities' rather than 'Icebreakers' because so many people say they 'hate icebreakers'. We've included them because they set the scene, help people relax, start off gently and, of course, break the ice!

HUMAN BINGO

An activity to get people moving around, talking to each other and finding out each other's names.

> 👤 10 – 100+ people

> ⚪ Time: 15 minutes

How does it work?

Everyone is given a 'Bingo' sheet divided into 16 squares (see sample pages at back).

Each square challenges you to find a number of people who fit into a certain category. For example:

> - Find three people who have had their photograph in a newspaper.
> - Find one person who has visited a country you have never been to.
> - Find two people who speak more than 2 languages (see sample pages at back).

You then go around asking people if they fit into the various categories and if they do, you write their name in the box.

The game is over when someone has filled all the boxes – Bingo! - or when you are ready to move on to the next activity!

Why do we like it?

- Not everyone arrives at the same time for an event. **Human Bingo** allows you to get things started with those who are there first and to get others involved as they arrive.
- You can choose categories that fit into a theme and change them for different settings.
- It gives everyone a reason to talk to each other.
- It gives everyone permission to talk to each other.
- You find other people with whom you have things in common.

What will you need?

- Bingo sheets made and photocopied in advance and pens for everyone.

© Dynamix 2002

When have we used HUMAN BINGO?

- At the start of an Ice-breaker Day for 150 new sixth form students.
- Play training events for 100+ summer play scheme workers.
- A school Environmental Awareness Day.
- Teambuilding for Dutch and English primary school children, Bristol.

Links to other activities

Feedback the results by getting everyone in a circle and use an activity such as **The Wind Blows** using the **Human Bingo** categories.

(NB: We refer to other activities in the book on most pages – there's a handy index to all activities in this book on page 140.)

Developments/Adaptations

- You don't have to have 16 squares; you could use 12 or 9 for example.
- Have a themed **Human Bingo** to set the scene for the kinds of issues you will be discussing. For example:

   The Environment
   Find three people who recycle things.
   Find two people who have planted a tree.
   Find one person who has picked up someone else's litter.

   Young People's Rights
   Find three people who have signed a petition.
   Find two people who have met their MP.
   Find one person involved in a school council.

- This activity obviously requires reasonable literacy skills. You could get everyone to work in pairs to support each other or use a similar, less wordy icebreaker such as **Human Treasure Hunt**.
- You could get really creative and make a Bingo Card with visual images to depict the category.

Menu

See Menus A, D, G and H.

© Dynamix 2002

HUMAN TREASURE HUNT

An activity to get people moving around, talking to each other and finding out names.

⋔ 10 – 100+ people

◯ Time: 15 minutes

How does it work?
On a flip chart write up a list of 'treasure' to find – and the treasure is people! For example:

A	Someone who has been swimming in the past week.
B	Someone who knows what the UN Convention on the Rights of the Child is.
C	Someone who watches Eastenders.
D	Someone who has passed their driving test.

Give everyone a piece of paper and a pen and ask them to find the 'treasure' in the room by asking people what they know, what they do and what they like. They should write the letters down and put the name of the person they find – the treasure! – next to the right one.

Why do we like it?
· It is quick to set up, and there is no photocopying.
· It gives people both a reason and permission to approach others and ask them questions.
· The treasure themes can be frivolous or serious.
· You don't have to write much.

What will you need?
· Flip chart or white-board and pen.
· Blank scrap paper and pens for everyone.

© Dynamix 2002

When have we used HUMAN TREASURE HUNT?

- Inclusive stall design training, Save the Children, London.
- Youth worker training, Gloucester.
- Play training of summer play workers.
- When there is not enough time to prepare a **Human Bingo**!

Links to other activities

Use the 'treasure' categories for **The Wind Blows**.

Developments/adaptations

- You can have as many pieces of treasure as you want to – eight is a good number - and a piece of treasure can be one person or any number of people, for example, three people who are vegetarian.

- You can draw symbols next to the treasure and read them all out at the start of the activity to help ensure inclusion of people with limited literacy skills.

- If people don't feel confident about writing you can tell the 'treasure' to write their own name on the other person's paper. This way you only ever have to write your own name.

Menu

See Menu L.

© Dynamix 2002

JIGSAW

Jigsaw can be used to get people into random groups. It works equally well as an icebreaker activity, team-building exercise or information gatherer.

♦ 10 – 100+ people

● Time: 15-20 minutes

(depending on jigsaw content)

How does it work?

Prepare a jigsaw of challenges in advance – see 'What will you need?' below and also the sample at the back of the book. Everyone gets a piece of jigsaw and then has to find all the other people with the same colour jigsaw piece as them. Once the pieces are put together, the groups can read and carry out the instructions.

Why do we like it?

- Jigsaw gets people into small random groups and talking to each other.
- If you set challenges which don't involve much writing you can keep the activity inclusive, because only one person needs to be able to read out the completed jigsaw.
- You can keep the challenges as simple 'getting to know you' activities. For example:

> - Write down everyone's name.
> - Each person draw a picture of your favourite food.
> - Draw a map of the local area and mark everyone's home on it.

Or you can open up more pertinent discussion – e.g. for a youth club:

> - Write down everyone's name and school.
> - List five important features of a youth club.
> - Collect a plan of the new youth club and write a list of good points and bad points and any changes you would make.

If extra people arrive late you can tear some jigsaw pieces in half!

© Dynamix 2002

What will you need?

- Jigsaws! Write or type your challenges on one side of A4 paper in fairly large print (see sample at back of book). Photocopy onto different coloured sheets. When you know how many participants you have (i.e. on the day they all arrive!) cut up the sheets into the appropriate number of jigsaw pieces. 40 participants? Then make five jigsaws, cut each into eight pieces, hand out and you have five random groups of eight people.
- You also need materials appropriate to the challenges you ask – flip chart paper, markers, scrap paper, coloured pencils etc.

When have we used JIGSAW?

- European Anti-Poverty Alliance: Conference for young people from all over Europe. One of their challenges was to draw a map of Europe and place their home town onto it.
- Preparation for work experience for a Swansea Secondary School - the challenge was to draw a map of Swansea and mark onto it their homes, work place, school, bus station and other local landmarks.
- Teaching and learning styles training – the challenge was to draw a picture of a brain.

Links to other activities

You can move on to any other small group activity or game, e.g. **Similarities and Differences, Post-its Ideas Storm.**

You can start **Opinion Finders** in these small jigsaw groups.

Developments/Adaptations

- Challenge the groups to make an image which can be stuck on the wall as a gallery, e.g. a map of the area with pertinent landmarks.
- Ask questions to get a snapshot of shared knowledge or opinions on something.
- Having stuck images up at the beginning of a session you can return to them at the end to see if any new knowledge has been gained – e.g. in the brain theory example above, students improved on their initial diagrams by the end of the training.

Menu

See Menus H and M.

© Dynamix 2002

ALPHABETICAL ARCHIPELAGO or ISLANDS

...you choose!

A game to get people moving and sitting next to different people.

- 10 – 100+ people
- Time: 10+ minutes

How does it work?

Get everyone to stand in a circle and give them a sheet of newspaper. Tell them to tear it in half and stand on one of the pieces. Ask them to do origami with the other half and make a shark by screwing up the paper and throwing it into the middle of the circle. You then tell them that they are no longer standing on a piece of paper in a room but are each on an individual island...an archipelago. But this is no ordinary string of islands, it's an alphabetical archipelago – so they have to get themselves in alphabetical order of first names with all the Angelas and Andrews at one 'end', and all the Zoes and Zacs at the other.

If they step in the water they will be eaten by the sharks so they must co-operatively move around the islands! You can put on your shark-proof boots and provide a piggyback service to help people if you want to (especially for large groups). You can put on a time limit if you want, e.g. two minutes. Check their success by sending a Mexican Wave round the circle as you call out the letters of the alphabet (they lift their arms as you say their letter).

Why do we like it?
- It usually makes people laugh.
- It moves people from sitting in their friendship groups.
- The Mexican Wave is a good energiser.
- It allows people to move around and make a noise between quiet listening times like welcomes and introductions.

What will you need?
- A sheet of newspaper for each person and a loud voice!

© Dynamix 2002

When have we used ALPHABETICAL ARCHIPELAGO/ISLANDS?

- Meeting of young people and National Assembly for Wales members, Llais Ifanc/Young Voice.
- 'Common purpose' course for managers of change.
- Mediation course for primary school.
- Youth Conference, Barnet, London.

Links to other activities

Having 'shuffled' the group, you can ask them to learn the names of the people on either side of them.

You can get them into pairs or small groups that are likely to be mixed (not fixed by gender or friendship etc).

In these pairs you could play **Reporters** or **Whose Hand is it Anyway?**

Developments/Adaptations

- You don't have to use newspaper, you can use chairs or just stand.
- You don't have to have sharks, you can make it okay to walk around.
- You can get into order of things other than alphabetical names, such as date of birth, distance travelled to get here, your house number (be prepared to give random numbers to people with only a house name! And find out the highest number before you do the Mexican Wave...you might need to count in hundreds!)
- You can send the Mexican Wave around a few times.
- You can make the Wave very small – lift a finger, or very big – stand up with arms in the air.
- You don't have to have chairs, you can stand.
- You don't have to make a circle, you can make a line from one end of the room to the other.

Menu

See Menus D and M.

© Dynamix 2002

REPORTERS

An activity where you speak to one other person and share information about yourself, then report your findings.

- 4 - 100+ people
- Time: 5 - 10 minutes

How does it work?
In pairs, ask people to give their names and some other information about themselves to their partner. For example;

> Tell your partner your name, what you had for breakfast,
>
> and what you think is the best thing about this youth club.

Give them two or three minutes to do this.

Get everyone back into a circle and ask people to report their findings about their partner to the group.

Why do we like it?
- The participants only have to talk about themselves to one other person. When they speak publicly they are talking about their partner, which is often easier – it is rare that someone won't even say the name of their partner.

- You can use **Reporters** to ask simple, gentle, even frivolous things, or you can include a question which starts to set the scene for issues to be discussed later in the session.

What will you need?
- Only some willing reporters!

© Dynamix 2002

When have we used REPORTERS?

- Promoting Co-operative Classrooms, primary schools, Toxteth.
- Meze Days – training for after-school club workers, Chwarae Teg, South Wales.
- Co-operative Learning Conference, Co-op College, Loughborough.

Links to other activities

Two pairs introduced to each other could then be a group for a **Post-its Ideas Storm**, or think up questions for **Hot Seating**.

Two groups of four, put together into groups of eight could lead into **Opinion Finders**.

Developments/Adaptations

- Instead of feeding back to the whole group you can get each pair to join another pair and each introduce their partner to the new pair. The group will then be in groups of four and will know each other's names, ready for another exercise!
- If you are working with a large group it would take too long for everyone to feedback to the whole group, so the above method allows everyone to report as well as give information. It can also be less intimidating than reporting to the larger group.
- Reporting in the large circle can be systematic or random, include everyone or just be voluntary. You need to judge your group. Some people might not be ready to speak to the whole group yet, even about someone else.
- If any of your group are visually impaired they may learn to recognise people by their voices, so **Reporters** could be run in pairs with individuals reporting back about themselves.

Menu

See Menus H, L and M.

© Dynamix 2002

THE WIND BLOWS

An information gathering exercise which is light-hearted and gets people moving around and sitting in different seats.

- **10 – 100+ people**
- **Time: 10 - 15 minutes**

How does it work?

The group sits in a circle (it's better with chairs, but can work without). The facilitator says, "the wind blows all the people who...(name a category!)". Anyone who fits into that category must stand up and be 'blown' to a different seat. You can encourage people to float on the breeze like a leaf, be a cool leaf that walks, or even an unenthusiastic leaf that doesn't move very fast or very far! Continue with the wind blowing different categories of people until the group is well shuffled.

Why do we like it?

Although people often look at us as if we must be joking when we suggest they get blown by a wind, we have never known this game to fail. If you pick a category you can see first (e.g. people wearing trainers) then peer pressure often gets people moving. Asking non-threatening questions like "people who like chocolate", "...who have a brother" or "...who have lived in this town all their lives" can help to create an atmosphere where it is easy to move. Pick topical categories like people who attended local sporting or music events. You can get a picture of the group by asking "who has attended consultation events before", or "who knows at least three other people in the room".

This game works in most settings with any number of participants. It can also work for more sensitive issues - 'the wind blows anybody who knows someone who....has been bullied, is lonely' etc. You can also ask useful questions like, "the big wind blows anyone who is a first-aider" or "...anyone with specific needs they want the group to know about" e.g. bad back, hearing impairment.

© Dynamix 2002

What will you need?

· Everyone in a circle.
· Some categories prepared in advance (on paper or in your head!)
· Somewhere to write down the results if you want – it might be useful to remember later that 90% had never been to an event before, 50% are smokers, or 80% know someone who is bullied.

When have we used THE WIND BLOWS?

· Under-fives Anti-Bullying Project, Swansea and Neath Port Talbot.
· Transition Training, primary and secondary Schools, Moray, Scotland.
· Lambeth Schools Parliament Day.

Links to other activities

The Wind Blows can be used to feedback activities like **Human Bingo** and **Human Treasure Hunt**.

After **The Wind Blows** the group will be sitting randomly in a circle ready for anything!

Developments/Adaptations

· Instead of moving round to a new seat, you can just step forward, maybe take a bow or wave when you fit into a particular category. This can be a useful adaptation if you have any participants who use a wheelchair.
· Making a point of getting people to identify those they have things in common with can help to break down prejudices.
· You can have themed ways of moving (e.g. modes of transport, animals, dinosaurs…)

Menu

See Menus A, C, D, E, F, G, H, I, J, K, L, M and N.

© Dynamix 2002

ZOMBIES

A name game.

 👤 10 – 50+ people

 ⬤ Time: 10 minutes

How does it work?
The group stands in a circle. Check that everyone knows what a zombie is and choose a volunteer to be the first 'zombie' – someone usually starts to walk like one any way! Get your zombie to put their arms out in front of them and fix their gaze on someone in the circle. The zombie must walk towards a 'victim' and if they touch them on the shoulders, the 'victim' becomes a new zombie.

The victims can only save themselves by shouting out the name of anyone else in the circle before the zombie touches them, so that the zombie will head towards that person instead.

Zombies and caught victims can swap places or just keep getting more and more zombies. The game ends when chaos takes over!

Why do we like it?
· The idea of zombies usually appeals to young people.
· The game makes people laugh! You can stitch up your friends by saying their name if they are right next to you.
· You also make sure you learn a few names before the game starts.
· It's funny and works well as an icebreaker!

What will you need?
· Everyone in a circle.
· Everyone needs to know at least a few other names before you start.

© Dynamix 2002

When have we used ZOMBIES?

· School Mediation Training.
· Promoting Positive Play Grounds in a Swansea Primary School.
· 'Put a Dinner Lady on the Roof' Anti-Bullying Project, Swansea and Neath Port Talbot.
· Conferences, especially if delegates are hung over!

Links to other activities

Usually the calm that follows the mayhem that is **Zombies** is a great space in which to introduce the next activity.

Developments/Adaptations

· You can start by making the zombie and victim swap roles until everyone has got the idea of the game, then increase the number of zombies.
· If people don't know each other very well you can help the zombie by getting the potential victim to point at their chosen alternative.
· Zombies can be very slow moving or quite fast if it's a big circle.

Menu

See Menu J.

© Dynamix 2002

SIMILARITIES AND DIFFERENCES

A small group game to help people realise they have a lot in common.

👤 10 – 60+ people

⏺ Time: 10 - 15 minutes

How does it work?

Ask groups of about six people to find a similarity that they all share, for example a food that they all like. Ask each group to feedback, then ask for more similarities. For example:

- A food none of you like.
- A local place you have all visited.
- A place you have all visited which is as far from here as possible.

You can then ask them to find differences such as 'a food you've eaten that no one else has tried', or 'a CD you own that no one else has'.

Feedback and point out how much easier it is to find similarities than differences!

Why do we like it?

- People soon discover that they have similarities to others despite the fact they are strangers, not in their peer group or usual friendship circle, or from a different area.
- The process of finding the similarities and differences gives people the opportunity to talk about themselves and make connections with others in the group.
- People usually end up laughing!

What will you need?

- Small groups – six is ideal, with more than eight it gets difficult!

© Dynamix 2002

When have we used SIMILARITIES AND DIFFERENCES?

· Mentor training, secondary schools, Swansea.
· Cardiff Youth Forum.
· Co-operative classrooms, Bristol schools.
· Celebrating 125 years of Co-operation, Rochdale schools.

Links to other activities

Can be used as an icebreaker for small groups once a larger group has been split. They should then feel more comfortable and relaxed to work together on more demanding activities.

Developments/Adaptations

· You can introduce an element of competition amongst the groups, for example, which group found a shared place they have all visited furthest from here, or who found someone who has eaten the most unusual food?

Menu

See Menu M.

© Dynamix 2002

WHOSE HAND IS IT ANYWAY?

A funny but quiet activity which requires concentration!

👤 10 – 30 people

⬤ Time: 10 minutes

How does it work?

Get the group into pairs and ask them to close their eyes and feel the hand of their partner. They need to pay attention to detail so that they can recognise the hand again.

Get everyone to open their eyes and wander around the room away from their partner. Say, "Stop – close your eyes...turn around on the spot" then challenge the group to find their partner by keeping their eyes closed and feeling the hands of others until they recognise their partner's hand.

Suggest they reject hands gently and have a few 'seeing' facilitators around the room to make sure no one walks into walls! Once they find their partner, they should open their eyes and move out of the way of the other players.

Why do we like it?

· This is a game that seems impossible until you play it!
· It is a quiet, slow-moving activity which requires concentration.
· No reading, writing or talking is required.
· You feel a strong shared experience with your partner – knowing their hand so well makes them easier to talk to!

What will you need?

· A group divided into pairs and a quiet start.

© Dynamix 2002

When have we used WHOSE HAND IS IT ANYWAY?

· Dim Prob, Student Community Action training, Aberystwyth.
· Swansea Youth Forum.
· Integrated Arts Workshops, South Wales.

Links to other activities

Other paired activities such as **Reporters** or create a **Discussion Carousel**. (Remember, if you want to find other activities in the book, check out the index on page 140).

Developments/Adaptations

· Instead of recognising the hand by touch, the pairs can invent a 'secret handshake'.
· Collect pairs of small objects and hand them out randomly. Get people to shake hands with their object in their palm until they find someone with the same object. You can play this version with eyes open or closed.
· Get everyone to think of a skill or hobby they have. They then write it on an address label and stick it to the palm of their hand. Challenge the group to find people they have something in common with by revealing their label to others as they move around.
· These adaptations are useful if you have members of the group who are uncomfortable with touching hands so intimately or who may not be allowed to because of their culture.

© Dynamix 2002

OPINION FINDERS

An information gathering exercise that allows you to find everybody's opinion on a number of statements.

♦ 5 - 100+ people

● Time: 20 - 30 minutes

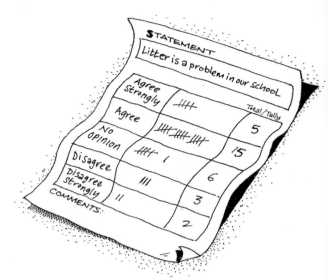

How does it work?

Everyone in the room is given a sheet of paper with a statement at the top. Beneath the statement there is a grid for recording people's opinions according to whether they 'agree strongly', 'agree', have 'no opinion', disagree' or 'disagree strongly' with it, and there is a space at the bottom for comments (see the template at the back of this book). There are a number of different statements and each statement is on different coloured paper.

Before you start the activity, make sure everyone understands his/her statement. Then get them to go and be 'opinion finders' by asking other people their opinions on their statement. The colour coding allows people to seek out statements different to their own. Everyone gives and collects opinions simultaneously. When someone gives their opinion the grid should be ticked next to their response. Encourage everyone to give their opinion on every statement. After about ten minutes get them to stop!

The next step is to gather together all those who have the same coloured sheets and to ask them to tally their results individually, then as a group. These results can be fed back orally for the facilitator to write up or written onto flip chart paper by the group.

Why do we like it?

- Everyone gives their opinion on a range of issues early on in an event.
- They only have to speak to one person at a time and it is a two-way process of asking and giving opinions.
- You can be more scientific by insisting that everyone gives their opinion on each statement only once.
- You can use the activity to get a big group into smaller mixed groups.

© Dynamix 2002

What will you need?

- A set of appropriate statements photocopied onto the **Opinion Finder** template (see back of book). Make sure they are clear and in a language which is appropriate for your group. Each statement must be photocopied onto a different coloured sheet.
- A pen for each person.
- Flip chart and markers to feedback.
- Masking tape or blue-tac to gallery results on the wall.

When have we used OPINION FINDERS?

- Children's rights outdoor event, Woodcraft Folk, Bristol.
- Consultation with Looked After Children: issues around the care system, Barnet
- Urban Regeneration Consultation (8-14 year olds): local issues, Clydach, Swansea.

Links to other activities

Opinions gathered at the start of an event can be used to inform later activities. For example, one of the statements the majority agreed with could form the topic for a **Discussion Carousel** to find out why.

Move onto another small group activity after the feedback.

Developments/Adaptations

- You can write each statement and grid on flip chart sheets and stick them up on the wall then ask people to go to each sheet and put a tick next to their opinion. This adaptation worked well to include young people with limited motor skills who used Bliss communication boards to give their opinions to their support workers who then wrote up their responses.
- You can create mixed groups by handing out randomly shuffled statement sheets at the start, or
- You can get the group into small groups first and hand out one colour of statement sheets per group, to ensure that everyone understands their statement. This also takes the pressure off for individuals who may not be able to read or understand the statement.
- If your group would struggle with the language of 'agree strongly', 'disagree' etc, you can use symbols such as ticks and crosses, smiley and sad faces or 'yes' and 'no'.

© Dynamix 2002

- Avoid negatives in the opinion statements and don't be afraid to be contentious! For example, say:

  'Bullying is a problem in our school' rather than
  'Bullying is not a problem in our school'
  'It is safe to play outside where I live' rather than
  'It isn't safe to play outside ...'
  'It should be legal to smoke from age eight' rather than
  'Smoking from age eight should not be ...'

- We have also used **Opinion Finders** to set the themes for large conferences.

Menu
See Menus A, B, C, D, E, F, I, J and L.

© Dynamix 2002

SECTION 7

Information Gathering and Promoting Discussion

The activities in this section are all useful for gathering the views and opinions of your group.

IDEAS AVALANCHE

A way to quickly gather ideas
from a group.

3 – 30 people

Time: 10 minutes

How does it work?
Set the topic for discussion and ask for
suggestions. As people call out their
ideas, write them up on a flip chart.
**It is crucial that you write down
everyone's suggestions to value them,
even if they seem impossible or
unrealistic.**

Once the **Ideas Avalanche** is over you can discuss which ideas are
most practical, whether any are impossible because of safety issues or
the law, and which ones should be discussed further.

Why do we like it?
· It is potentially a quick way to get lots of ideas.
· The whole group can see, hear and be inspired by the ideas as they
  are shared.
· As long as you create a safe space and really do value all
  suggestions, then people tend to let their imaginations run and
  often come up with many creative ideas.

What will you need?
· Flip chart and markers.

© Dynamix 2002

When have we used IDEAS AVALANCHE?

- We almost always use an **Ideas Avalanche** in our 'Making it Work' session (i.e. setting ground rules) at the beginning of any work we do with any group. See page 15.
- 'What makes a good reward in school?' – Promoting Positive Behaviour in Schools, Swansea.
- 'What happens if you don't learn?' – Salford Anti-Truancy Project.
- 'Key issues for a healthy school' – Iechyd Morgannwg Health.

Links to other activities

You can gather ideas for the **Hot Air Balloon** or collect categories to prioritise for **Diamond Ranking**.

Developments/Adaptations

- If you feel people are excluded from this activity through shyness or over-enthusiastic participation of others, then you could use **Post-its Ideas Storm** instead.
- If no one puts forward ideas, suggest a 'murmur' time where everyone talks to the person next to them for a minute to see if they can come up with something together.
- You can deliberately take suggestions from different areas of the circle to prevent one person from dominating.

Menu

See Menus C, F, G, L and M.

© Dynamix 2002

POST-ITS IDEAS STORM

An information gathering exercise
done in small groups.

⦿ 3 – 100+ people

⦿ Time: 15 minutes

How does it work?
Divide into groups and give each one some post-it notes and a pen. Write the question to be discussed up on a flip chart, for example:

> * What should be the aims of a Youth Forum?
> * What makes a good Youth Worker?
> * What makes a good Playground?

Then ask the groups to write their ideas onto post-it notes – one idea per post-it. Facilitators collect the post-its as they are generated and stick them onto the flipchart, clumping similar ideas together. Once all the ideas are collected, feed them back.

Why do we like it?
* Everyone has the opportunity to contribute their ideas.
* You don't have to say what your idea is in front of the whole group.
* Only one person per group has to write – this can be a facilitator.
* Clumping similar ideas together makes shared issues stand out.
* If each group has different coloured post-its they can see their ideas contributing to the whole picture.
* If you want to know who wrote what, you can note which group had which colour.
* You can easily move the post-its around on the big sheet!
* It looks nice!

What will you need?
* Different coloured post-it notes (or different coloured pens if you can only get yellow ones!)
* Pens, flip chart and markers.

© Dynamix 2002

When have we used POST-ITS IDEAS STORM?

- 'What can I do to help the Environment?', Rochdale environmental awareness event.
- 'What makes a good Head teacher?' Primary School, Scotland.
- 'Who should we invite to our conference?' Swansea Youth Forum.
- 'What is Bullying?' anti-bullying training course.

Links to other activities

Use this activity to generate ideas for **Diamond Ranking** or **Dot Voting**.

Explore some of the issues with **How How How**. For example, one of the popular ideas generated by a **Post-its Ideas Storm** on 'What should be the aims of a Youth Forum?' was 'to represent all local young people'. You could then run **How How How** asking 'How can we get all local young people represented in the Youth Forum?'

Developments/Adaptations

- If you are working with a small group, they can work in pairs.
- Write a big list of issues as you feedback ideas, with 'scores' to highlight the more recurrent ones.
- Ask for only five ideas per group, prompting a discussion about the ideas before they get written down.
- You can stick the post-its onto an image, e.g. draw around a young person and run a **Post-its Ideas Storm** on children's rights.
- Stick the post-its directly onto a chart.
- You can allow people to draw visual images if they prefer that to writing.

Menu

See Menus A, B, C, D, H, I, J, K, L and M.

© Dynamix 2002

DISCUSSION CAROUSEL

A way to discuss an issue which allows everyone to give their own opinions and listen to others on a one-to-one basis.

6 - 50 people

Time: 20 minutes

How does it work?

Get everyone to move their chairs so that they make two concentric circles, the inner one facing out and the outer circle facing in. There should be the same number of people in each circle so that everyone is facing someone who they can talk to (see diagram). Set up a topic for discussion, e.g. How can we improve behaviour in schools?' or 'What should the local council be doing for young people?' Give everyone a minute to consider their views then give the inner circle one minute to tell the person sitting opposite what they think. The outer circle must listen and not speak.

Then swap over so the outer circle speaks while the inner circle listens. Then move people around; i.e. get the inner circle to move one seat clockwise and the outer circle to move one seat anti-clockwise. Now ask the inner circle to explain what their previous partner's views were, in 30 seconds, and then do the same with the outer circle. They can then express their own views to this new partner so that each person has four sets of ideas to consider: their own, and those of their first and second partners, and their second partner's partner.

Why do we like it?

· Everyone has to express their views on a subject but they only have to speak to one other person at a time.
· People are encouraged to listen to the opinions of others as well as expressing their own.
· People have to repeat other people's views. This can be very powerful, especially in a mixed adult/young person group when adults have to express the views of a young person and vice versa.
· A minute isn't too long if you don't feel you have much to say.

© Dynamix 2002

What will you need?
- Chairs for everyone and a watch or clock.
- A large diagram of the two concentric circles often helps!

When have we used DISCUSSION CAROUSEL?
- Planning for a play area, politicians and young people, Oxford.
- Youth Unemployment Conference, young unemployed, councillors and senior civil servants, Port Talbot.
- Staff Development – Communication and Feedback Review, primary school, Swansea.
- Aggression management courses, identifying examples of aggressive behaviour.

Links to other activities
Feedback from **Discussion Carousel** can inform a debate, having allowed people to explore the issues first. You can run a **Value Continuum** before or after a **Discussion Carousel**, or do both and see if people have changed their views.

Developments/Adaptations
- You can move around again.
- Collect feedback by gathering the inner and outer circles into two groups and getting them to tell you what they heard.
- Vote on a topic, then run a **Discussion Carousel** on that topic. Vote again and see if the views have changed.
- The inner circle can think of a problem or situation with which they are struggling. The outer circle can provide suggestions for solutions. Move the circle around again to allow people to gather more solutions.

Menu
See Menus A, B, D, E, F and I.

© Dynamix 2002

VALUE CONTINUUM

A means of exploring sensitive issues and
allowing non-verbal expression of views, which
can be used to initiate discussion.

- 👤 5 - 20 people (all on the line)
- 👤 6 - 100+ people (sending delegates)
- ⬤ Time: 5 - 25 minutes

How does it work?

Set up an imaginary line across the room, clearly
marking where it begins and ends (with chairs,
for example, or masking tape on the floor). Then
explain that this line is a continuum with two opposing views at each
end: e.g. one end could be 'I love to eat meat, I eat it at every meal',
while the other end could be 'I am vegan, I believe meat is murder and
I campaign against the meat trade'. Having set up the two extremes,
ask people to stand on the line according to their opinion. In this
example, the vegetarians would be nearer to the vegan end, fish-
eaters near the middle, while people who don't eat red meat would be
beyond them, and your cannibals would be close to the other end! You
can allow people to verbally express their opinions once they are all on
the line, or just move on.

Why do we like it?

- You can quickly get a feel for where a group are in relation to an
  issue.
- You can have this exercise up your sleeve to help you decide the
  direction in which to go with your discussions.
- If people find it intimidating to stand on the **Value Continuum** you
  can adapt it to make it less threatening.
- You can ask about anything as long as you can set up two extremes.
  When enthusiasm was fading within a youth conference planning
  group, we had views ranging from, "this conference is a waste of
  time, let's all go home" to "this is going to be the best youth
  conference the world has ever seen". This allowed those with
  enthusiasm to share it and those with fears and doubts to express
  them, and left the group feeling like they had made the choice to
  continue together.

© Dynamix 2002

What will you need?

- A way of marking the ends of the continuum, and to have thought through your two extreme positions.

When have we used VALUE CONTINUUM?

- Avoiding Drugs Solutions: harm reduction, risk assessment, Swansea Schools.
- Behaviour, sanctions and rewards, Pupil Referral Unit, Swansea.
- Exploring values on inclusion and attainment, Scottish Schools Learning Alliance.

Links to other activities

Any activity which explores issues in more depth, such as **How How How** or **Cotton Bud Debate**.

You could repeat the value continuum after further discussion to see if people's views have changed.

Developments/Adaptations

- Get people into pairs or small groups of three or four. Ask them to discuss their position and send one representative to the continuum.
- Place objects on the continuum instead of standing on it, e.g. a small group sitting round a table placed pennies on a line on the table. Once, one young person who had been very reluctant to participate threw his baseball cap to one end of a continuum to express his views. The rest of the group then joined in by placing caps or shoes on the line, making the whole situation more relaxed and inclusive.
- Bring the two opposing ends of a continuum round to speak to each other and put people from the middle in the same group so that people with extreme and neutral views talk to each other.
- You can use a rope with knots in it or with ribbons tied to it to include people with visual impairment.
- If the concept of a continuum is too complicated, you can use two mats – one for 'yes', one for 'no'. You could also include a third to represent 'maybe' or 'don't know'

Menu

See Menus C, D, E, F, I, J, K, N and M.

© Dynamix 2002

ARTY MURAL

A way for people to express themselves through visual arts.

👤 1 – 20+ people

⚪ Time: 20 minutes

How does it work?

Set a topic or theme for the mural, for example 'What young people in this area do in their free time' or 'The best playground ever'. Then encourage people to express their views on that topic by drawing pictures and images.

You can get them to work individually and stick all the pictures together on a wall in a collage, or have a very large piece of paper for everyone to gather around and work on together.

Why do we like it?

- There is no reading or writing involved.
- The process of deciding what to do gets the groups talking about the issue.
- You can start with easy, potentially funny topics and then move on to more serious issues.
- It is easier for people to take part, as they don't have to act, just pose!

What will you need?

- A large roll of paper – wallpaper, print roll or similar.
- Any combination of paint, paintbrushes, pallets, markers, pencils, felt-tips. You can also use scraps of fabric, tin foil, sweet wrapper etc to make a collage – then you need glue too!
- Sponges, deodorant rollers and body parts all make interesting effects.
- Something to protect the floor!

© Dynamix 2002

When have we used ARTY MURAL?
- 'Dreams and nightmares for the future'
  – Children in Wales Conference.
- 'Smoke Bugs' – anti-smoking work with primary school children.
- 'Images of young people around the world'
  – Red Cross Youth Consultation.
- 'Reasons to bomb Merthyr and reasons to save it'
  – Merthyr Youth Conference.

Links to other activities
Ideas from the mural can lead onto further discussion.

Equally the mural can follow on from more wordy activities.

Developments/Adaptations
- You can work on the mural on a wall or on the floor.
- You can fix images to a large piece of fabric to make a banner or backdrop.
- The mural could be an ongoing activity during an event.
- You can choose whether words are allowed or not!
- Graphics can be transferred to publicity material, e.g. 'Have Your Say Day for Looked After Children' in Dudley made bookmarks with images from their murals.
- You can use the mural for evaluation.
- If you want more words you can call it a graffiti wall – you may need to agree rules on keeping it positive or at least not personal.

Menu
See Menus E, G, M and N.

© Dynamix 2002

FREEZE FRAME

A physical activity creating visual
images like a 'snapshot'.

3 – 20+ people

Time: 20 minutes

How does it work?

Get into small groups of about five
to seven people and challenge them
to pose in a freeze frame of a
scene. Give them a theme such as,
'Young people enjoying themselves'
or 'A time when a young person has received help in a difficult
situation'. They should use their imaginations first to decide as a group
what they are trying to depict and then devise a way to represent it
as a freeze frame.

Another way of explaining **Freeze Frame** is to suggest they act out a
scene and then freeze in character.

Have a 'showing' time where groups take it in turns to show their
Freeze Frame while others try to guess what's going on.

Why do we like it?

· No reading or writing is involved.
· The process of deciding what to do gets the groups talking about
  the issue.
· You can start with easy, potentially funny topics and then move on
  to more serious issues.
· It is easier for people to take part, as they don't have to act,
  just pose!

What will you need?

· Small groups.
· To have thought about some possible themes beforehand.

© Dynamix 2002

When have we used FREEZE FRAME?

· Evaluation session with young people who interviewed the Children's Commissioner for Wales: freeze frame the best moments of process.
· Avoiding Drugs Solutions: show a situation and freeze frame a potential solution.
· Children's Rights Conference – exploration of the United Nations Convention on the Rights of the Child: freeze frame a right that children have.

Links to other activities

Can link to any other small group activity, using the **Freeze Frame** to set the scene.

Developments/Adaptations

· Groups can challenge each other to make different scenes.
· This activity can be used to present ideas to an audience.
· You can use props.
· You can use **Freeze Frame** as an evaluation method by asking for the best or worst moments of an event.
· You can take photos so that you have a record of the ideas.
· Groups can do a series of freeze frames to tell a story (captions are optional!)

Menu

See Menus E and G.

© Dynamix 2002

DOT VOTING

A method of prioritising a
series of ideas.

♦ 10 – 100+ people

● Time: 5 - 10 minutes

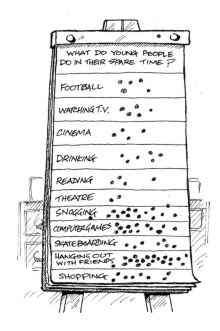

How does it work?

Create a list of possible answers in
response to a question or statement
on a flip chart – for example, things
young people do in their spare time.
Leave some space next to each
answer. Give everyone three sticky
dots and ask them to place their dots
next to the three activities they do
most often. You can all see
immediately which activities are the
most popular.

Why do we like it?

·   It is a very quick method of voting.
·   You can give people one or more dots.
·   You don't have to talk about your choices.
·   Your vote is anonymous.
·   There is a very clear visual image once voting has taken place.

What will you need?

·   A big list of ideas.
·   Dots for everyone.

© Dynamix 2002

When have we used DOT VOTING?

- 'What do you do out of school?' using pictorial images of free time activities, Oxford Play Consultation.
- 'What stops you learning?' – Burry Port Motivation Day.
- 'Where do you get information?' – Swansea Youth Conference.
- 'What is your favourite reward?' – Promoting Positive Behaviour Project, Swansea.

Links to other activities

Use other consultation methods to create the list of ideas, e.g. **Ideas Avalanche, Post-its Ideas Storm, Discussion Carousel, Arty Mural.**

Developments/Adaptations

- Dot Voting can be used to determine which issues to focus on.
- You can restrict people to one vote each.
- You could use visual images to depict the ideas so that no reading is necessary - this would require advance preparation.
- You can colour code the votes to see if people vote differently according to age, gender, adults/young people, geographical area, etc.

Menu

See Menus D, L and M.

© Dynamix 2002

PAPER CAROUSEL

An information gathering exercise in small groups.

⚹ 6 – 30 people

● Time: 20 - 30 minutes

How does it work?

Split the group into three. Give each group a piece of flip chart paper with a subject or question at the top, for example:

> • Why do people bully others?
> • What effect does bullying have on people's lives?
> • What can be done to stop bullying?

Give each group five minutes to write down their idea on their sheet, then move the pieces of paper round. Give each group another five minutes to read the ideas already on the sheet, ticking the ones they agree with. Then ask them to add their own ideas. Continue the carousel by moving the sheets round so that every group has seen each question and has had the chance to add their ideas to each list. Finally, pass the sheets back to their original groups and feedback or display the lists.

Why do we like it?

- It is a structured way to get everyone to consider a series of issues.
- You work in small groups so information is often shared more freely.
- Only one person per group has to be confident about writing down the ideas – this can be a facilitator.
- Ideas are not repeated – you can just tick the ones you agree with.
- It generates a fairly concise list of everyone's ideas on a subject.

What will you need?

- Flip chart paper and marker pens.
- To have thought of a number of clear subjects around which to gather ideas.

© Dynamix 2002

When have we used PAPER CAROUSEL?

· Preparing an anti-bullying workshop: origins, effects and solutions for bullying, conference planning, Townhill and Mayhill Young People's Group.
· Implications of brain science research for classrooms, Suffolk teachers' 'inset' day.
· Promoting Positive Behaviour project, looking at responsibilities of different people in school.

Links to other activities

Ideas generated by activities such as **Post-its Ideas Storm** can be considered in depth.

Developments/Adaptations

· You can use Paper Carousel as an evaluation tool with headings such as:

    What was the most useful thing about today?
    What was the most unexpected thing about today?
    What would you change about today?

· If you have a large group you can run two or three carousels simultaneously with the same issues.
· Three is an ideal number of questions – four is okay. Any more and it can get tedious.
· You may want to use tokens (see **Cotton Bud Debate**) so that each person in the group has the opportunity to make a point on each issue.
· If you have been sitting for a long time, ask the groups to carousel around fixed sheets of paper.

Menu

See menus A, B, D, E, G, I, J and N.

© Dynamix 2002

COTTON BUD DEBATE

A technique to give everyone in a
group an equal chance to speak.

† upto 30 people

● Time: 5 minutes+

How does it work?
Give everyone three cotton buds
(or other tokens such as beads) and
set up a subject for debate, e.g.
'What is unacceptable behaviour?'

Every time someone speaks (this can
include speaking to a neighbour!)
they must hand over a cotton bud to
the facilitator (a hat or box is useful for collecting them). Also, if
someone speaks for a long time they can lose two or even three cotton
buds in one go.

Another facilitator can write up points from the discussion on a flip
chart to keep track of what's being said.

Why do we like it?
· Everyone has equal opportunities to speak.
· Confident speakers cannot dominate the discussion.
· There is no reading or writing involved – the facilitator's notes can
  be read aloud at the end to ensure everyone's points are included.
· People don't have to speak, they can hand over a cotton bud to show
  their agreement with a point being made.
· Less confident speakers have been known to hand over buds to
  people they trust to make points for them.

What will you need?
· Enough cotton buds/beads/tokens for everyone to have three each.
· Something to collect them in.
· Flip chart paper and marker to write up points.

© Dynamix 2002

When have we used COTTON BUD DEBATE?
- 'What support services do we need?' – Bristol Young Carers
- 'How can we promote participation?' – Local Government Information Unit, London.
- 'How can we promote learning?' – Salford schools
- 'What do you want to do in your youth club?' – Treboeth Youth Club

Links to other activities
- **Cotton Bud Debate** can be used to facilitate participation in other activities such as **Ideas Storm** or **Paper Carousel**.

Developments/Adaptations
- This activity does not have to be planned – if a discussion arises naturally and you want to encourage everybody to speak, then this is an ideal method.
- You can always have this activity up your sleeve to give everyone a chance to speak on a subject.
- You can give each person one token and wait until everyone has had the chance to say something before you begin an open discussion.
- You can use sweets as tokens – people eat their sweets once they have made a point.
- As you gather any remaining tokens, be open to collecting more suggestions - very shy people have been known to whisper their idea to the facilitator at this point.
- Saboteurs can collect the tokens or be 'snitch police', making sure people give up a token when they speak, even to their neighbour.

Menu
See Menus D, E, H, I, K, M and N.

© Dynamix 2002

HOT SEATING

An activity which enables individuals to share information without being put in the spotlight.

- 👤 5 – 50 people
- ⏺ Time: 5 - 10 minutes

How does it work?

Introduce an empty chair as 'the hot seat'. Put something on the hot seat and ask questions about it. It can be/represent a person but not any specific individual. For example:

> - You could put 'A youth worker' on the hot seat and ask questions about being a youth worker, which any of the youth workers present could answer, but you don't put anybody specific in the spotlight.
>
> - You could also put something like 'The School Council' on the hot seat - the idea, not the members themselves - so anyone can ask a question of the school council and anyone in the school council can answer.

Why do we like it?

- No individual has to be in the spotlight or know all the answers.
- Answers can come from anyone in the group, or an 'expert' group.
- **Hot Seating** is a very versatile information sharing activity which also works well as an icebreaker – we often put 'Dynamix' on the hot seat and allow participants to ask questions about our organisation as an alternative introduction to sessions.
- One person can take the hot seat and imagine how another individual might answer and so experience some empathy for their point of view.

What will you need?

- A seat!
- A way of showing what's on the hot seat - such as a leaflet, document, or a sign (e.g. saying 'School Council').
- It can be useful to have an easy or less abstract example with which to introduce the idea of **Hot Seating** . We often use a puppet and answer on its behalf. People ask questions such as where it lives, what it eats, and if it has a girlfriend.

© Dynamix 2002

When have we used HOT SEATING?

- 'A Bar of Divine Chocolate' – Inset for teachers, social workers and community workers, Scotland.
- 'The City of Greece' – Primary school, Bournemouth.
- 'The Old Bloke Down the Road' – Ground Work Trust, Rhondda.

Links to other activities

You can use **Hot Seating** to determine the level of knowledge on a subject, so that you can pitch other activities to explore any gaps or differences of opinion.

Developments/Adaptations

- You can challenge people to ask difficult questions.
- You can get people to devise questions in pairs or small groups.
- You can make **Hot Seating** more dynamic by getting whoever is answering the question to run and sit in the seat while they give their answer.
- You can put individuals on the hot seat if they are confident and feel comfortable to be there, but you do need to set some rules about their choice to answer certain questions or not.
- You can make it into a 'detectives' game by sitting in the hot seat and not revealing who you are, for example:

    "I am going to answer questions as if I were a form of contraception. Ask me questions until you can name me!"

- You can use **Hot Seating** to give information:

    "I am an Equal Opportunities Policy – find out as much as you can about me in five minutes."

    In the two adaptations above, the facilitator in the hot seat must answer questions on behalf of the thing they represent, and not as themselves.

- You can test the knowledge of your group by telling them to ask questions to which your answer would be 'yes'.

Menu

See Menus B, D, E, G, H, K, L and M.

© Dynamix 2002

SECTION 8

Involving Children and Young People in Long Term Planning

This section describes methods which can be used to explore a subject in more detail. They are particularly useful when working with groups over a longer period of time, especially for planning sessions. However, most of the activities can be used in a wide range of settings.

How How How

An activity which allows you to explore an issue in more depth or to break it down into smaller issues.

- **20 people max**
- **Time: 20 minutes**

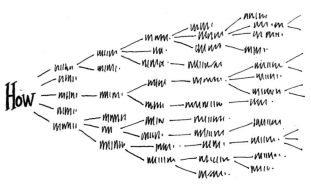

How does it work?

Write a 'How...?' question on a long, wide piece of paper and draw four or five arrows coming from it. Ask the question, and write down any suggestions at the end of the arrows. For example:

'How can we get more young people involved in the Youth Forum?'

Explore these suggestions in more detail by asking "How...?" again. People might suggest, "Talk to them about it." You must then ask "How?" again, to which they might answer "Go to where they meet and give a talk", "Tell your friends", "Tell people in the street". You need to ask "How?" again to each of these... "How can we tell people in the street?" to which they might answer, "Give out leaflets", "Stop them and do a questionnaire" and so on.

Why do we like it?

- You can break a problem/task down into smaller issues/tasks.
- You can use **How How How** for action planning to determine what needs to be done and who will do what.
- If you treat **How How How** as an **Ideas Storm** and use the rule that every idea counts, you can even explore more 'off the wall' ideas which may lead you to exciting places and to some dead ends!

What will you need?

- A long wide sheet of paper – we use print roll, the back of wallpaper or two pieces of flip chart joined together.
- Markers.
- A 'How...?' question.

© Dynamix 2002

When have we used HOW HOW HOW?

* 'How can we stop bullying?' – Anti-bullying work, Swansea. This resulted in an answer which became the title of the project, 'Put a Dinner Lady on the Roof'.
* 'How can we stop vandalism of empty council houses?' – The Knowledge Course for housing officers, Swansea.
* 'How can we improve transport for young people?' – Greater Manchester Passenger Transport Executive.

Links to other activities

Generate ideas using **Post-its Ideas Storm**, **Ideas Avalanche** or **Paper Carousel** and ask 'How...?' about any of them!

Developments/Adaptations

* You can also ask, "What...? What...? What...?"
  e.g. 'What happens if you don't learn?'
* You can also ask, "Why...? Why...? Why...?"
  (but beware of getting the response, "DELILAH!!")
  e.g. 'Why do young people misbehave in school?'
* You can set up small groups to work on individual ideas.

Menu

See Menus A, B, H, J, L and M.

© Dynamix 2002

DIAMOND RANKING

An activity to help people to set priorities together.

> **groups of 4 - 8**

> **Time: 20 minutes**

How does it work?
Set a question and have nine ideas for people to prioritise. For example:

> 'What should the police spend its money on?'
>
> Ideas:- Reducing terrorism, crime, mugging, drugs, burglary, sexual assaults, violence.
> Fast response, protecting children.

Write each idea on a post-it note and ask each group to arrange their nine ideas in a diamond shape (as above) with their top priority at the top, two in second place, three in third place, two in fourth place and the lowest priority at the bottom. They need to get a consensus as a group and can move the ideas around until they reach an order with which they all agree.

Why do we like it?
- The groups discuss the issues without it feeling like a discussion.
- Post-it notes allow the ideas to be moved around again and again.
- Even if someone hasn't got views on all the issues, they usually have an opinion about the importance of some of them.
- It encourages people to justify why certain issues are more important in their opinion.
- You can compare diamonds and collate results even across different groups at different events.
- You can give clear information to service providers, for example about what service users believe the spending priorities should be.

What will you need?
- Post-it notes and pens.
- Flip chart paper with a diamond layout drawn on to it.

© Dynamix 2002

When have we used DIAMOND RANKING?
- Policing priorities, Hackney Metropolitan Police and young people.
- Budgeting priorities, Council Cabinet, Swansea.
- 'Skills needed to be a peer supporter' – Assist, Anti-smoking project.
- 'Skills needed to be a prefect' – prefect training, Salford.

Links to other activities
You can use other information-gathering exercises to establish the nine ideas to prioritise (e.g. **Ideas Avalanche**, **Post-its Ideas Storm**, **Dot Voting**, or **Discussion Carousel**).

You can explore the top priorities further using **How How How** or Discussion Carousel.

Developments/Adaptations
- You can prepare some of the ideas in advance on post-its. Give each group blank post-its with which to add their own ideas, then get them to prioritise all nine.
- Feedback the results after the event by scoring five points for being in the top box, four points for the second row, three for the third row, two for the fourth row and one point for the bottom box.
- You can collate results further by running the same activity in different schools and feeding back or displaying all the different results to initiate further discussion.
- We often feedback the top three ideas for each group for instant comparisons of the top priorities.
- A facilitator working with a group of blind young people used Lego blocks with Braille instead of post-its.

Menu
See Menus A, C, D, F and I.

© Dynamix 2002

TALKING STICK

A way to give everyone an
uninterrupted opportunity to speak.

5 - 30 people

Time: 10 minutes +

How does it work?
Introduce an object that is to be
your 'talking stick'. The idea is that
whoever has the talking stick is the
only person who can speak. When
they have finished expressing their
views they pass the talking stick on
to anyone else who would like to speak.

It should never just be passed around the circle – this can be
intimidating and daunting for many people, as well as making someone
feel so worried about their impending turn that they are unable to
listen to what others are saying. **Talking Stick** is as much about
everyone listening as it is about the person talking.

Why do we like it?
· It is a light-hearted way to get everyone else to keep quiet while
  one person speaks.
· It is often easier to express your views if you feel confident that
  you will not be shouted down or interrupted.
· People always choose to take a turn with the talking stick – they
  shouldn't be put on the spot.

What will you need?
· An object to be your talking stick – we have used a stick, a marker
  pen, a large shell, a toy microphone, a plastic duck, a puppet and a
  toy 'sheep of happiness'!

© Dynamix 2002

When have we used TALKING STICK?

· 'How did you get on with your funding application?' – Housing Officer training.
· 'Reasons to use this pack' – Parenting Order Course Conference.
· 'What strategies do you already use in your work?' – Under-five's Anti-Bullying Training.
· 'What shall we do about...' – Circus Eruption, Integrated Youth Circus.

Links to other activities

Talking Stick is another activity like **Cotton Bud Debate** which you can either plan to use as a specific exercise or have ready as a tactic. It can be useful as a tactic because it gives everyone the opportunity to express their views during an impromptu discussion or even during an activity like **Ideas Avalanche** or **Value Continuum**.

Developments/Adaptations

· You don't have to pass the stick on, you can just return it to a central point each time, for someone else to pick it up.
· If you are working with a group of people who feel comfortable with each other, you can pass it around the circle so that each person has a turn. This can be a useful way to feedback from an earlier session if people have been asked to do something in between.
NB: You should still give people 'permission' within the activity to pass the stick to their neighbour without saying anything.
· We have passed round a top hat so that whoever is wearing it can speak.

Menu

See Menu M and N.

© Dynamix 2002

HOPES AND FEARS IN A HAT

An activity which allows people to express their hopes and fears anonymously.

⚫ Any number of people

⚪ Time: 10 mins + 10 mins feedback

How does it work?

Give everyone two pieces of paper. Choose a topic, and ask them to write down their hopes about the topic on one sheet, and their fears on the other. Explain that they do not have to write their name. For example:

> - Hopes and fears about the future for young people in this area.
> - Hopes and fears about today's session.
> - Hopes and fears for this Youth Forum.

Have two collection hats – one for hopes, one for fears – and collect all the pieces of paper in them. Once you are away from the group, i.e. during a break, write up a list of all the hopes and a list of all the fears.

Later in the session or even at a follow-up meeting, feedback the two lists. It is important to address all the issues in order to value everyone's contributions. On some occasions you may need an outside person to help clarify issues or address fears.

Why do we like it?

- People are usually honest – and sometimes braver! – when they know their contribution is anonymous.
- It is useful to see the collated lists. Some hopes and fears are shared by many. Some people's fears are other people's hopes and vice versa. These are all useful starting points when planning together.
- You can plan the content of follow-up sessions to address people's fears.
- You can use the hopes to foster positive attitudes.

© Dynamix 2002

What will you need?
- Scrap paper and pens for participants.
- Flip chart paper and markers for writing up the hopes and fears.
- Hats or other containers in which to collect the hopes and fears.

When have we used HOPES and FEARS IN A HAT?
- Hopes and fears for the play schemes, play training.
- Hopes and fears about going to secondary school, Moray Primary School, Scotland.
- Hopes and fears for the future, Bristol Young Carers.
- Hopes and fears about being a mediator, mediation training.

Links to other activities
You can use the hopes and fears generated to plan other activities.
Run a **Discussion Carousel** on a shared fear. Run **How How How...** can we make a particular issue less of a worry for people?

Developments/Adaptations
- Instead of hats, use other imagery such as a wishing well with a bucket hanging inside and a dark cloud with a bucket underneath (our cloud had a cheesy silver lining!) We then ask for wishes and worries rather than hopes and fears.
- If your group has low literacy skills they could work in pairs (though this does make it less private).
- You can just do **Fears in a Hat**.

Menu
See Menus L and M.

© Dynamix 2002

WORLD'S WORST

A way to highlight issues by exploring them in their negative extreme.

♦ 5 - 30+ people

● Time: 20 minutes

How does it work?

Think of a situation or role you want to explore and challenge the group to describe the 'world's worst' version of it, for example, the 'world's worst meeting' or the 'world's worst social worker'.

Collect ideas by writing them up on flip chart paper. Then use these ideas to identify the issues that need to be addressed. You can then move on to finding solutions to the problem. For example:

In the world's worst meeting, 'only adults who have loud voices and are at the front get to say anything'.

Issue   Meetings should be organised so that everyone who wants to express an opinion has the opportunity.

Solution   When we set up meetings we should use participative activities so that everyone is included.

Why do we like it?

- By confronting a situation or role in its extreme, difficult elements are expressed as caricatures of themselves and are easy to ridicule and often funny.
- People can reveal painful truths in a light-hearted atmosphere.
- It is a fun way to get to serious issues.

© Dynamix 2002

What will you need?
· Flip chart and markers for writing up ideas.

When have we used WORLD'S WORST?
· 'The world's worst consultation' – Dynamix consultation methods training.
· 'The world's worst residents' meeting' – 'The Knowledge', housing officer training.
· 'The world's worst care review meeting' – National Children's Bureau, working with looked after children.
· 'The world's worst training' – School's Council Training.

Links to other activities
Once you have described the 'world's worst' something, you could make a **Freeze Frame** of it. Alternatively small groups could make a **Freeze Frame** first and then you could use their ideas to generate one big list describing the 'world's worst'.

You can take the list from the **World's Worst** to plan strategies to deal with each issue. Use **How How How** to study issues in more depth or create **Top Tips** to share with others.

Developments/Adaptations
· Act out the situation or role with the facilitator playing the part of the young person. This worked well when we played the part of a young person attending a care review meeting. Young people acted as the panel of adults and were able to reveal a lot of information that could later be explored with them. The empathy of the facilitator was intense after this experience too!
· Create a pictorial image of the world's worst using pens, paints etc.

Menu
See Menu M and N.

© Dynamix 2002

TOP TIPS

A way to consolidate your work on an issue into an easily digestible list!

30+ people

Time: 10 minutes

BABY SITTING
- BE SOBER
- DON'T BRING YOUR VICIOUS DOG
- LIKE CHILDREN

How does it work?

Having spent time exploring an issue or generating ideas around a subject, challenge the group to come up with a list of top tips for that issue or subject. For example:

> After running a series of activities to promote good listening, ask the group to make a list of 'Top tips for good listening'.
>
> Having set up a youth forum, get the group to reflect on what they have done by creating 'Top tips for setting up a youth forum'.

Why do we like it?

- It works well as a participative way to review what has gone before.
- Top tips lists can be shown to members of the group who are absent, incorporated into future sessions or used to plan peer education. For example, 'Top tips on setting up a youth forum' could be used by forum members as a starting point for planning the training of other youth forums.
- It is easy to type up and keep as a record of what happened!

What will you need?

- Flip chart paper and markers.
- Scrap paper and pens if you want to work in smaller groups first (see Developments/Adaptations).

© Dynamix 2002

When have we used TOP TIPS?

- 'Top tips for a good consultation' – Dynamix consultation methods training.
- 'Top tips for communication' – mediation training.
- 'Top tips for looking after volunteers' – volunteering conference.
- 'Top tips for being a Dad' – fathering conference.
- 'Top tips for running a conference' – The Hill Young People's Group, Swansea.
- 'Top tips for running games' – play training.

Links to other activities

After looking at the **World's Worst**, the group could be inspired to make **Top Tips** for making the Worlds' Best (See our cartoons!)

You could use **Post-its Ideas Storm** to gather the top tips or run it as an **Ideas Avalanche**.

Developments/Adaptations

- Ask for Top Ten Tips (sounds good and you can always add more than ten if you have more ideas!)
- Work in small groups to generate some top tips then gather everyone's ideas together.
- Make a mnemonic, for example:

  Fun
  Open
  Representative
  Unprejudiced
  Mouthpiece

- Young people could work out a set of **Top Tips** to make a more positive set of rules, e.g. **Top Tips** for making our youth club a safe place for everyone. Then write them up and stick them on the wall for everyone to share.
- You could ask for ten commandments.
- You can turn the **Top Tips** into a flip chart sized book.

© Dynamix 2002

SWOTT

A way to evaluate a group or
event which can help to
structure future planning.

📍 it depends

⚪ Time: 20 minutes

How does it work?

SWOTT stands for Strengths,
Weaknesses, Opportunities,
Threats and Training.

Set your topic and then consider
each element in turn. For example:

> 'The local council's recent consultation event aimed at
> young people'
>
> In this case you would consider the strengths of the
> consultation, any weaknesses, any opportunities arising from
> it, any threats the group perceives for its continuation or
> follow-up, and finally any training issues they can identify.

You can gather this information in various ways. Work on all five
headings (strengths, weaknesses, opportunities, threats, training)
in small groups, run an **Ideas Avalanche** or **Post-its Ideas Storm**
on each element in turn, or run a **Paper Carousel** of all the
headings simultaneously.

Why do we like it?

· It is a useful structure for breaking down an evaluation process.
· Asking for strengths and weaknesses encourages people to think
  about what has gone before. Opportunities and threats encourage
  people to look to the future. Training is another way to ask, "what
  do **you** need?"
· You end up with lists of ideas you can follow up or use to structure
  future planning sessions.

© Dynamix 2002

What will you need?
It depends on what methods you use to gather information
(see list on previous page).

When have we used SWOTT?
· School Council, Swansea Secondary School.
· Central Team, Red Cross.
· Volunteering, International Year of Volunteering Conference,
  Preston.
· Conference Evaluation, Swansea Youth Forum.
· Staff training and teambuilding, secondary school.

Links to other activities
You can use any of the methods suggested to carry out the
SWOTT analysis.

You can also explore any of the issues raised in more
depth using **How How How**, or **What What What**
(e.g. What What What... can we do about the threats?)

You could also follow **SWOTT** with **Hopes and Fears in a Hat**.

Developments/Adaptations
· Change the words!

Strengths	what was good?
Weaknesses	what was bad?
Opportunities	what could happen now?
Threats	what might stop things happening?
Training	what help do you need?

· Use the lists of ideas to write a report or make recommendations.
· Use the ideas to plan the next steps for the group.

© Dynamix 2002

HOT AIR BALLOON

A structured way to gather information together to facilitate planning.

♦ groups of 4 - 8 people

● Time: 20+ minutes

How does it work?

Draw a picture of a hot air balloon on flip chart paper. Make it large enough to write on, and include the balloon, basket and ropes tethering it to the ground. Tell your group that this balloon represents their organisation or project. They should then think about issues around the future of the project as follows:

1. **Who needs to be on board?** On the basket or on the people, write the names of the people or organisations who need to support the project in order for it to go anywhere, e.g. young people, workers, funders.
2. **What needs to be in place for the project to take off?** On the balloon itself, write factors and issues which need to be sorted in order for the organisation to fly, e.g. a building, staff, constitution, resources.
3. **What is holding it back?** Next to the tethering ropes write factors which are preventing the growth of the project, e.g. no funding, no support from local community.
4. **What will really make it fly?** Above the balloon write factors that will really help the project to grow, e.g. enthusiasm, commitment, good planning.
5. **What might blow the balloon off course?** Either side of the balloon – representing the winds that could buffet the balloon about - write down factors which could be problematic for the project once it is off the ground, e.g. continued funding, key young people leaving.

If you have several groups working simultaneously on balloon pictures, compare them and use the ideas gathered as a springboard for planning.

Why do we like it?
- The image is easy to understand.
- It is an interesting visual tool which encourages discussion.
- It helps to identify issues which need to be confronted.
- There is scope for comparison across different groups.

© Dynamix 2002

What will you need?
- One picture of a hot air balloon on flip chart paper for each group. You could also use smaller photocopied versions (see back of book).
- Coloured markers.

When have we used HOT AIR BALLOON?
- 'Setting up a mentoring course' – Mentor Training.
- 'Implementing the United Nations Convention on the Rights of the Child in your workplace' – Pembroke.
- 'Encouraging participation in learning' – Inset for education professionals, Moray, Scotland.

Links to other activities
Look at any issues raised in more depth using **How How How**.

Prioritise the things which need to be in place using **Diamond Ranking**.

Developments/Adaptations
- Use a series of exercises to answer the five questions then summarise the results on one large balloon picture. You could use:
  Ideas Avalanche
  Discussion Carousel
  Post-its Ideas Storm
  How How How...can we make it fly?
  Cotton Bud Debate
- Work in small groups then compare your ideas. If you have a mixed group of adults and young people then split them into adults only and young people only groups for interesting comparisons.
- Plan future training sessions according to what needs to be in place or what will make it fly.
- If you don't like the balloon image, try a different form of transport...a ship, a bus, even a bicycle could work!
- Go one step further and get on a rocket, then explore starting afresh on the new planet you land on.
- You can add a notice board to your picture and get groups to design a logo for their project.

Menu
See Menus J and M.

© Dynamix 2002

LIFELINES

An activity for individuals which encourages personal reflection.

♦ ♦ ♦ ♦ groups of 4 - 8 people

● Time: 20+ minutes

How does it work?

Give everyone a blank lifeline sheet (see back of book).

Explain that the lifeline starts from the moment they were born and continues until today. Ask the group to think of significant moments in their lives according to your theme. For example:

> A light-hearted icebreaker-type theme might be 'TV programme you liked to watch.' Individuals would then write down their favourite TV programme at different ages along the line.

A more serious theme might be 'Things you were allowed to decide for yourself'. This would be a way to start thinking about participation and understanding Article 12 of the United Nations Convention on the Rights of the Child. You could then compare lifelines in pairs or make a giant lifeline and gather any ideas from around the group that they are willing to share.

Why do we like it?

- You can do the activity on your own and not show anyone else.
- Team building can happen unexpectedly when people find they have shared experiences.
- You can get a perspective on an issue from different age groups.
- You can play **Lifelines** just for fun or use them to inform decision-makers. For example, asking a group of older teenagers to make a **Lifeline** about significant play experiences could inform playground planners of the kinds of equipment and stimulation children need and prefer at different ages.

© Dynamix 2002

What will you need?
A blank **Lifeline** and a pen for everyone.

When have we used LIFELINES?
· 'Important transport experiences' – consultation with young people, Greater Manchester Passenger Transport Executive.
· 'Important experiences' of the disabled delegates – Transition to Adulthood Conference.
· 'Toys you remember' – Play theory training icebreaker.

Links to other activities
You could play **Similarities and Differences** around the theme.

You could keep **Lifelines** personal but then ask a question about a specific age and run an **Ideas Avalanche** or **Post-its Ideas Storm**. For example:

Lifeline: Important play experiences.
Ideas Avalanche: What kinds of activities do 8 – 10 year olds like?

You could use the Lifeline as thinking preparation for a discursive activity like **Cotton Bud Debate** or **Discussion Carousel**. For example:

Lifeline: Things you were allowed to decide for yourself.
Discussion Carousel: What decisions should children be allowed to make?

Developments/Adaptations
· The lifeline can be narrowed down, for example: 'the past two years', 'since you started school' or 'from the time you stopped living with your parents/carers'.
· You can do a lifeline of a group or organisation, e.g. 'map the history of this youth forum along a lifeline'.
· You can look to the future and set starting and finishing points such as 'from now until you retire', and ask 'what will be your spending priority?' or 'what will you do in your spare time?'
· You don't have to use the template – get people to draw it themselves!

© Dynamix 2002

NEWSPAPER HEADLINES

An activity to get groups to focus on key information about an issue and make a noise!

> 👤 groups of 3 - 6 people

> ⬤ Time: 15 minutes

How does it work?

Challenge each small group to invent a newspaper headline about your subject. They should try to get across the key issue and draw people's attention to their story. You can limit them to a maximum of ten words.

Once they have worked out what the key information should be, and have devised their headline, they should write it up in large letters on flip chart paper and be prepared to shout it out like a newspaper seller!

Why do we like it?

- It helps groups to focus on key issues.
- The discussion leading up to the production of the headline is as important as the headline itself.
- Everyone has a chance to shout if they want to! Shouting together can be a good energiser after lots of intense discussion!
- The headlines can be stuck on the wall to inspire further ideas and to help keep the focus on key issues.

What will you need?

- Scrap paper and pens for working out the headlines.
- Flip chart paper and markers to write them up.
- Blue tac or masking tape to display them on the wall.

© Dynamix 2002

When have we used NEWSPAPER HEADLINES?

- Workshop feedback, Youth Conference 2000, Swansea.
- 'Things we've done, things we're proud of' – Children in Foster Care.
- Workshop feedback, Workers' Education Association Conference.

Links to other activities

You could use a headline as a title for an **Arty Mural**.

You could use **Diamond Ranking** to establish what the key issues are before you make up the headlines.

You could run a **Cotton Bud Debate** on 'What are the key issues?'

Developments/Adaptations

- Write an article to match the headline.
- Write a press release.
- Make the headlines for TV news and act out an illustration of what you are talking about as a **Freeze Frame** or action scene. Work in larger groups and have a newsreader, reporter and actors.
- You can use **Newspaper Headlines** as a quick way to feedback from different discussions or workshops.
- You can end a session with this activity and create a Big Ear (see Menu K, page 131) to represent whoever you are going to give the gathered information to. The newspaper headlines could summarise the vital information for this ear to hear.

Menu

See Menu K for the adaptation, 'Big Ear', described above.

© Dynamix 2002

SECTION 9

Evaluation and End Games

This section describes a mixture of evaluation and end game activities, some of which are physical, some that require writing and others that don't, and some which work equally well during a session as well as at the end!

EVALUATION TARGETS

A quick, non-verbal evaluation tool.

♦ any number

● Time: 5 minutes

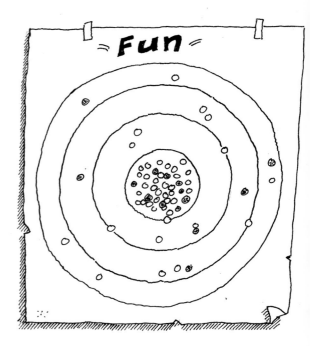

How does it work?

Draw a target (three or four concentric circles) on a piece of flip chart paper. Write an evaluation question at the top, for example:

> * Was today fun?
> * Did you feel listened to?
> * Would you come to another day like this?

Make a different target for each question. Give everyone sticky dots – one per target. Then ask them to stick one dot on each target according to how close to the centre their response would go. You might need to explain with examples such as, "If today was so much fun that you've really enjoyed yourself, then put your dot in the middle. If it was okay but not brilliant then put your dot further out. If you'd rather have gone to the dentist, then put your dot on the outside edge".

Why do we like it?

* It's really quick to set up and to run.
* You get a very clear image of the success of your session.
* People don't have to write anything and only have to read a few words, which will have been read out anyway!
* If you stick the targets around the room, people can have one last run about before they go home.

What will you need?

* Flip chart paper and markers to make the targets in advance.
* Enough dots for everyone to have one per target/question.
* Scissors to cut strips of dots.

© Dynamix 2002

When have we used EVALUATION TARGETS?
· In almost every piece of work we do.
· A teacher in one school used **Evaluation Targets** as a strategy for evaluating lessons.
· Youth Conference for International Co-operators (delegates from across the globe) – International Co-operative Alliance.
· Police Consultation, Hackney.

Developments/Adaptations
· If you forget your dots you can always leave a few markers next to each target and people can draw a dot – only for emergencies though!
· You can save paper by dividing your target into quarters and having one quarter per evaluation question.
· You can put a space for comments and a pen under each target so people can choose to give you written feedback too.
· You can give different groups different coloured dots so you can analyse the feedback from, for example, males and females, adults and young people, or representatives of different groups.
· A facilitator with the RNIB made three dimensional words at the top of the page and made the whole target tactile with ridges.

Menu
See Menus A, B, C, G, J and M.

© Dynamix 2002

WEB

A quiet, ending activity which encourages positive feedback to individuals.

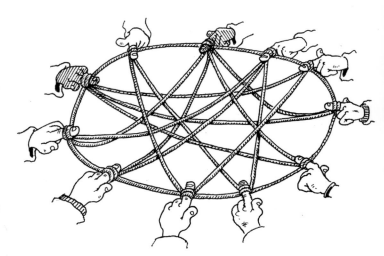

♦ 15 people max

● Time: 10 - 15 minutes

How does it work?
The group sits in a circle and the facilitator ties the end of a ball of wool around his/her finger. S/he then rolls the ball of wool to someone else in the circle and makes a positive comment about them. This person then wraps the wool around their finger before passing the ball of wool on to someone else while saying something positive about them. The process continues until everyone has wool around their finger and is part of the web.

Passing the wool once around the perimeter of the web, you can then reflect and say profound things about the time you have spent together. The final comment should be that it is now time for you all to leave, but that you will all take something away with you. You then cut the wool next to each person, breaking the web but leaving everyone with a symbolic strand of wool wrapped round their finger for them to take away with them to remind them of the things they have done, shared, learned etc.

Why do we like it?
· Although it sounds a bit cheesy when you describe it, this is a very powerful end game.
· We have returned to an event the following year and people have shown us the wool they took away last time.
· It creates a space for **everyone** to receive some positive feedback.
· It is visually beautiful and the symbolism – although corny! – is very true and easy to grasp.

© Dynamix 2002

What will you need?

· A big ball of wool and some scissors so you can release yourselves!

When have we used WEB?

· Play training day, Banbury.
· Communities that Care residential, follow-up meeting.
· Children's Rights Conference, London.

Developments/Adaptations

· You can ease the pressure on individuals having to say something by allowing anyone to say something positive abut the person who has just received the wool.
· You can run a web where people talk about their personal experience – for example, 'describe what the best part of the event was for you or something you'll never forget'.
· A web of thanks can allow each individual to thank someone else or the group for something.

Menu

See Menu L.

© Dynamix 2002

APPLAUDION CHAIR

A loud and energising
end game.

⋔ any number

● Time: 5 - 10 minutes

How does it work?

Introduce a chair as 'The
Applaudion Chair'. Explain that
if anyone sits on the chair it
will cause everyone else in the
room to cheer and applaud
enthusiastically. Demonstrate
by sitting on the chair. As
soon as you stand up the noise
should stop. You may need to
practise this! If people are
not enthusiastic and loud
enough then adjust the
'volume button' on the back.

Then offer anyone else the opportunity to sit on the chair. They can
sit on it for a moment or a long time, or they can bring a friend or
they can just place their hand on it...the possibilities are endless!

Why do we like it?

· See preceding paragraph!
· Some people never receive applause for anything
· How often do you receive enthusiastic applause for doing nothing
  other than sitting on a chair?
· We like to watch people glow when they sit down.
· The applause and adulation only last as long as you choose to sit
  there.
· If you really don't want a go, you don't have to have a go!
· If you think someone deserves a special vote of thanks, you can
  encourage them to sit on the chair.

© Dynamix 2002

What will you need?
- A chair.

When have we used APPLAUDION CHAIR?
- 'The Future's Purple' Conference for 200+ people, Scottish Human Services Trust.
- Inclusive Circus Workshop, Parasol Project, Oxford.
- Under-five's anti-bullying project.

Developments/Adaptations
- You can decorate the chair, drape it in cloth, or tie balloons to it.
- You can carry the chair to people who don't want to make the journey to it.
- You can make the **Applaudion Chair** status spread to every chair in the room so that everyone applauds everyone else (remember to switch it off again though!).
- If you haven't got a chair, or if some people would feel excluded by having to sit on one, you can use an Applaudion Mat.
- If someone uses a wheelchair you can turn that into the **Applaudion Chair**.

Menu
See Menus G, M and N

© Dynamix 2002

STONES IN A POND

A game which can be used for evaluation, making commitments or gathering ideas for next steps.

👤 any number

⬤ Time: 10 minutes

How does it work?

Make a symbolic pond – ideas below! Give everyone a 'stone' shaped piece of paper and a pen and ask them to write something on it, for example 'what will you do as a result of today?' Once they have written their ideas on the 'stone' they should drop it in the pond. When everyone's stones are in the pond you can talk about the ripples that one small stone can make, and encourage everyone to remember what they have written and to put it into action.

Why do we like it?

- It is a strong visual image.
- It encourages people to make at least one commitment.
- You don't have to write very much.
- It draws an event to a close.
- You can type up what's written on the stones as a record of the actions inspired by your event and refer back to them at future events.

What will you need?

- A pond! We have made them from blue paper cut into a pond shape, and have also used a blue plastic ground sheet. Each time we have added reeds, frogs and lily pads!
- Stones! We have cut stone shapes from brown, yellow and cream thick paper.
- You can put the pond on the ground, but we once made a display of ours by hanging it on the wall.

© Dynamix 2002

When have we used STONES IN A POND?

- 'Commitments and hopes for the future' – Swansea Youth Conference 1999.
- 'What can you do about children's right to live without violence?' – Save the Children Fund Global Partnership Stall. Ideas were contributed throughout the event.
- 'Hopes for the future' – Council for Voluntary Services Conference.

Developments/Adaptations

- The imagery of stones, ponds and ripples is especially good for commitments and next steps. We have used other images such as a wishing well - everyone was given a cardboard penny and asked to write a wish for the future of young people in their area.
- You can ask evaluation type questions, for example:

  What will you remember most about today?
  What was the most unexpected thing?

- We also once made a 'wishing tree' and people tied images and descriptions of their wishes for the future on to it.

Menu
See Menu I.

© Dynamix 2002

WHOOH! RATING

A very quick and noisy
evaluation and feedback game.

> 👤 any number

> ⬤ Time: 2 minutes

How does it work?
Ask the group to respond to
your questions with a
"WHOOOOH!" sound. The
loudness and enthusiasm of
their "whooh!" should
correspond with how positive
their response is.

So for example, if you asked,
"Have you felt listened to
today?" someone who may
have felt excluded or disempowered may make no noise at all. People
who felt they had been listened to would make a loud enthusiastic
"whooh!" noise. It's not very scientific! But it's quick and it gives you an
idea of the group's feelings at the end of a session.

Why do we like it?
·   It takes very little time. We first invented **Whooh! Rating** when we
    were told that a session had to end ten minutes earlier than
    anticipated, so we only had two minutes left!
·   Making a loud communal noise is energising and people tend to leave
    on a high.
·   Although **Whooh! Rating** doesn't give you much negative feedback, it
    does encourage people to reflect on aspects of the session such as
    how much fun they had, if they worked hard, and if they would
    attend again.
·   You can combine this with a more detailed written evaluation.

What will you need?
·   A few questions ready in your head!

© Dynamix 2002

When have we used WHOOH! RATING?

· School Teaching and Learning Styles day, Swansea.
· Workshop feedback, Swansea Youth Conference 2001.
· Choosing between options, training for dealing with challenging behaviour, Moray, Scotland.
· Choosing a name for the circus, Circus Eruption, Integrated Youth Circus, Swansea.

Developments/Adaptations

· You can wave your arms Mexican Wave-style indicating a 'whooh!-ometer' rating (lift them high for a resounding "yes!" and keep them down for "no!")
· You can feedback on other activities during an event.
  For example, the rest of the group could give a **Whooh! Rating** to **Newspaper Headlines** or **Freeze Frames**.
· If you are not up to a "whooh!" then you could clap.

Menu

See Menu K.

© Dynamix 2002

SIT ON MY KNEES PLEASE!

A co-operative end game
which can include everyone.

† 12 - 100+ people

○ Time: 10 minutes

How does it work?

This game needs to be run
safely. We have decided to
describe it as a list of
instructions which you could
follow word for word the first
few times you play this game!

- Everyone stand in a circle,
  shoulder to shoulder.
- Point your left arm into the circle.
- Turn so that your left arm is still pointing to the centre but you are
  now behind someone in the circle, not next to them.
- Take a small side step towards the middle.
- Lower your arm.
- Check you are still in a circle – no corners!
- Now hold on to the hips of the person in front of you.
- Now hold on to the hips of the person in front of the person in
  front of you.
- You should be very close together now and still in a circle.
- In a moment we will sit down on each other's knees. To keep us all
  safe we have a "Stop!" rule. If anyone is in pain or falling over they
  should shout "Stop!"and we will all stand up.
- Practise shouting "Stop!"
- So that we all sit down at the same time we will say together,
  "Sit on my knees please!" and **then** sit down.
- Don't think about sitting down, think about guiding the person in
  front of you onto your knees. Keep your knees together so they
  have somewhere to sit!
- If we all work together this will work!
- On a count of three, say together, "Sit on my knees please!" then all
  sit down.
- If you are comfortable you can lift your arms (advanced version!)
- All stand up together.

© Dynamix 2002

Why do we like it?

· It doesn't always work first time! But when it does work there is an amazing feeling of achievement.
· People find it hard to believe that it will work so like the best magic it is even more thrilling when it does.
· You can make a 'sitting circle' with a mixture of large, small, heavy and light people. The weight is spread so that no-one is taking the weight of one individual (you may need to reassure larger and smaller members of your group!)
· You can play **Sit On My Knees Please** indoors or outside.
· You can include a lot of people (our top score is about 250 in a field at Glastonbury festival!)

When have we used SIT ON MY KNEES PLEASE?

· School assembly to show 'We miss you when you're not here' – Salford Anti-Truancy Project.
· School's Council training day.
· Meze Days training for after school club workers.

Developments/Adaptations

· Put your arms in the air once you've sat down.
· Wave!
· Cheer!
· Smile!
· Do it again!

NB: Not everyone likes to be this close to other human beings so while you may need to gently encourage people to join in, always make it okay to opt out. Roles to keep people included are 'circle monitor' – making sure the circle has no corners – 'chant director' – count everyone in to say "Sit on my knees please!" – or even 'audience', ready to applaud and cheer if you manage to do it!

· If you think your group would like a more serious problem to solve you can tell them that Napoleon's soldiers kept themselves alive on the retreat from Moscow through thick snow by resting like this rather than freezing on the ground!

Menu
See Menu L.

© Dynamix 2002

POSITIVE FEEDBACK

An activity that builds self esteem and encourages positive feedback.

> **up to 20 is ideal, more is okay**

> **Time: 10 minutes**

How does it work?

Give everyone a piece of paper and a piece of masking tape. Ask the group to help each other stick their paper on their backs. Give everyone a pen (felt tips are the best). They should then go around writing positive comments on each other's backs. They may write messages of thanks, comment on contributions the person has made to the group, remind them of a moment they shared together, in fact anything at all that is nice and positive!

When everyone has had enough time to collect a good list of praise, stop the activity and let the group help each other to remove their lists and read them.

Why do we like it?

· People often keep these sheets of paper for a long time.
· It is beneficial to practise finding positive things to say about other people, even those you don't know so well.
· With careful facilitation there should be a good spread of feedback. We usually encourage everyone to find something to write on every other person's back.

What will you need?

· A blank sheet of A4 paper for each person.
· A pen – preferably a felt tip – and masking tape for each person.

© Dynamix 2002

When have we used POSITIVE FEEDBACK?

- End of twenty-week course, 'The Knowledge', with senior housing officers.
- Staff Development day, Faculty Centre, Brighton.
- After the annual show, Circus Eruption, Integrated Youth Circus.

Developments/Adaptations

- You can start the game in pairs so you can help each other to stick the paper on, then write on each other's backs before moving on to other people.
- Instead of sticking the paper to your back you can write your name at the top and leave it on your chair. Then everyone moves around the chairs to write their positive comments.
- You can play it a bit like 'Consequences' – write your name at the top of the paper, and pass it on. At the bottom of the sheet you have just received, write a positive comment about the person whose name is at the top, fold it over so no one can see what you've written and pass it on. Keep going until you get your paper back, all folded up with positive feedback inside!

© Dynamix 2002

LETTER TO YOURSELF

A quiet, personal activity which encourages people to make commitments and plan next steps.

♦ any number

● Time: 10 minutes

How does it work?

Give everyone a sheet of A4 paper, an envelope and a pen. Ask them to write today's date at the top and start a letter to themselves, 'Dear Me...'. Give them the beginning of three sentences for them to finish, for example:

> Dear Me
> Today I attended ...
> It has made me think about ...
> By the end of the month I will ...

Once they have filled in the blanks they should sign the letter, put it in the envelope, address it to themselves andthen give it back to the facilitator. In one month's time, the facilitator must post all the letters so that people get a reminder of what they thought about and what they intended to do.

Why do we like it?

· People often get very inspired at training or consultation events but then have to return immediately to their usual routine. **Letter to Yourself** is a gentle way to remind people of their good intentions.
· You can make contact with someone again for very little cost.
· Writing the letter gives people time to reflect on their experiences.

What will you need?

· Blank paper for everyone.
· A pen and an envelope for everyone.
· Flip chart and markers to write up the beginning sentences - or you can make a template letter and photocopy it beforehand.
· To keep the letters safe and remember to post them when you said you would.

© Dynamix 2002

When have we used LETTER TO YOURSELF?

- Young people looking at vocational options, Motivation Day, Burry Port.
- Adults working with children and young people, Children In Wales Conference.
- Promoting positive staff relations, Swansea School Staff Development Day.

Developments/Adaptations

- You can ask for all sorts of information to go in the letter, for example:

  What was the most unexpected thing about today?
  What was the funniest thing?
  What will you tell your family about today?

- You can focus on next steps, for example:

  In the light of today's event...
  ...what will you do in the next week?
  ...what will you do in the next month?
  ...what will you do in the next six months?

Menu
See Menus H and M.

© Dynamix 2002

ESTEEM TRAIN

A physical end game to leave
everyone feeling relaxed!

> ♦ 8+ people

> ⬤ Time: 10 minutes

How does it work?

Everyone stands in a circle. All turn
to your left so you are standing
behind someone. Stretch your
fingers. Gently massage the
shoulders of the person in front of
you. Feel free to give your
masseur/masseuse verbal feedback!
For example, "More!" "Mind my
neck, it's a bit sore", "Down a bit",
or "Ooh, lovely!"

After a few minutes give them physical feedback by all turning
the other way and massaging the shoulders of the person who has
just massaged you. End by gently stroking the shoulders and float
off happily!

Why do we like it?

· It makes people feel good.
· **Esteem Train** can provide a safe, relatively non-threatening
  opportunity to make physical contact with other members of the
  group. This can encourage team building and make people feel more
  comfortable with each other.

NB: **We say 'relatively non-threatening' as some people are very
uncomfortable with any physical contact. Always make it okay not
to join in. This activity works best when groups know each other
fairly well and have shared time and experiences together.**

© Dynamix 2002

What will you need?

- Agreed 'ground rules' about listening to the person you are massaging, not hurting them and making the esteem train a positive experience for everyone.
- To feel comfortable yourself. If you don't think this activity is appropriate... don't use it! Listen to your instincts and do something different.

When have we used ESTEEM TRAIN?

- Play training.
- Youth Conference planning team.
- To end an 'Anger and aggression management' training day.

Developments/Adaptations

- You can say encouraging words together whilst massaging. For example, after a long session with a youth forum planning team we all reassured each other by saying things like:

  Everything's going to be fine, we don't need to worry,
  We can run this conference!

  This combination of words and actions helped to calm some of their nerves before they went home.

- If people do not want to join in, you can get them to massage themselves – faces, temples, foreheads, their own hands.
- Everyone can just massage themselves and share a quiet moment of relaxation.

© Dynamix 2002

LAUGHING BELLIES

An end game to make everyone laugh!

- **up to 20 people**
- **Time: 10 minutes**

How does it work?

The first person lies on the floor. The next person lies with the back of their head on the first person's belly! Their two bodies make a 'T' shape like the diagram above. Person number three lies with their head on the belly of person number two, parallel with person number one – yes, you really need to look at the picture! – and so it goes on.

Once everyone is in position, person one says "Ha!" Person two says "He He!" Person three says "Ha Ha Ha" and so the laughing begins.

If you have a 'giggler' in your group make them number one person! The game dissolves into laughter and can go on for ages!

Why do we like it?

- The main purpose of this game is to make everybody laugh together.
- Laughter is a great way to release tension.
- Laughing together is a very positive way to celebrate the end of an event.
- No only do you get to laugh, but you get to lie down too!

What will you need?

- Enough floor space.

When have we used LAUGHING BELLIES?

- Dynamix Planning Weekend.
- With actors, puppeteers and circus workers, Portugal.
- Play training.

© Dynamix 2002

SECTION 10

Added spice

Quick and easy methods to spice up a session if groups need boosting or energising.

COUNTING TO TEN

A game for focusing and listening.

- Groups of 6 - 10 people
- Time: 5 minutes

How does it work?

Each group of six to ten people stands in a tight circle. Challenge them to count to ten. Every person must say at least one number and the numbers must be said randomly, i.e. they cannot just go round the circle or set up codes or signals. They must listen and be aware and be prepared to take a turn. If two people speak at the same time the group must start again.

Why do we like it?

- It is so simple, yet often so difficult! It is rare that a group can do this straight away and the group sense of achievement is high once they reach ten.
- You can challenge groups who get to ten to do it again with their eyes shut, or backwards!

KNOTS

A physical game which promotes co-operation and concentration.

- Groups of 6 - 8 people
- Time: 5 - 10 minutes

How does it work?

Each group of six to eight people stands in a tight circle. Each person places their hands into the centre and closes their eyes. Each hand must link with another hand - there can be no spare hands or groups of three! Once the links are made the group open their eyes and try to undo their knot without letting go of each other's hands. This will involve manoeuvring under arms and legs, making gaps big enough to pass through and very high levels of co-operation! The aim is to become a circle again. Sometimes the way links were made leaves you with two circles, sometimes interlinked – as long as the 'knot' is untied, it doesn't really matter!

Why do we like it?

- **Knots** gets people up and moving! It really doesn't work unless you co-operate, so there is a great sense of group achievement when the knot is unscrambled, yet it's still good fun if you can't quite unknot yourselves.

© Dynamix 2002

- We have adapted **Knots** to include someone with a broken arm by giving them a ribbon to hold instead of holding hands.
- If such close physical contact is inappropriate for your group you can all use ribbons or ties to make the links.

ON THE BANK IN THE POND

A game to promote good listening. Good for re-focusing after a break.

10 - 50 people

Time: 5 - 10 minutes

How does it work?
Get the group into a circle, kneeling on the floor and facing inwards. You, the caller, explain that for this game there are four positions:

On the bank	- hands on your knees
In the pond	- hands on the floor
The judge	- standing up and looking serious
Judging	- pointing at the accused

The game is a very simple version of 'Simon Says'. People must get into one of two positions, 'On the bank' or 'In the pond' according to which one you call. If anyone is not in the right place (i.e. on the bank when they should be in the pond or vice versa!) then they become a judge.

Judges stand on the edge of the circle watching carefully and point accusingly at anyone who is in the wrong place! Judges decisions are final. The game continues until there are only a few people left – those who are obviously good at listening but taking the game far too seriously! Applaud them and move on.

Why do we like it?
- It's really simple.
- Everyone stays part of the game – if you are 'out' then you get a higher status role.
- If people are getting too good at being in the right place you can add a rule, 'Do as I say, not as I do', then try to confuse them by being in the opposite position to the one you just said. That should get rid of a few from the circle!
- There doesn't have to be an outright winner, in fact it's better to stop the game when there are a few champions for the judges to applaud!

© Dynamix 2002

FRUIT SALAD

A moving-around game which can help to split a large group.

- 20 - 40 people
- Time: 5 - 10 minutes

How does it work?
The group sits in a circle and you name them all individually as one of four groups – e.g. apple, orange, pear or banana. One person (it could be you) stands in the middle and calls the name of one of the fruits. If you shout "Apple!" then all the 'apples' change places, or if you shout "Banana!" all the 'bananas' move. The caller can also shout "Fruit Salad!" at which everyone changes places.

Why do we like it?
- The caller can join in, sitting down on an empty seat when others are moving so that a new person is left in the middle.
- Groups get 'shuffled' by the process and you can move on to a more formal activity using mixed groups by suggesting all the apples work together, or all the oranges etc.
- You can use other themes – exotic fruits, TV characters or contraceptives, for example. You would then need a new command to make everyone move – for example if your groups were 'the pill', 'the condom', and 'the morning after pill' then the command could simply be "Contraception!" or "Sex!"

CATERPILLARS

A fast-moving, fairly physical game.

- 15 - 40 people
- Time: 5 - 10 minutes

How does it work?
Get the group sitting in a circle, preferably on chairs. One seat is left empty and one person is in the middle of the circle. When the game starts one person next to the empty chair moves onto it, and the person next to them moves into their vacated chair, and then the next person moves on...like a caterpillar. The person in the middle tries to sit on an empty chair before the next bit of the caterpillar sits on it. If they do manage to sit down, the person who should have sat on that chair moves to the middle and the caterpillar sets off in the opposite direction.

© Dynamix 2002

Why do we like it?

- It's fast-moving without running around and the facilitator can shout "Change direction!" to liven things up!
- People playing **Caterpillars** need to concentrate, move and work together. They also usually laugh – all good activities to both relax and stimulate the mind!

HUGGY BEAR/CLUMPS

A game to get people into groups and raise awareness of things they have in common.

- **10 - 100 people**
- **Time: 5 - 10 minutes**

How does it work?

If the facilitator calls "Huggy Bear threes" people get into groups of three; "Huggy Bear sixes" mean groups of six etc. "Huggy Bear your shoe size" means get into a group with all the people who wear the same size shoe as you. "Huggy Bear the month you were born" means a group who share the same month as you. How you form your group depends on the people you are playing with! You can call this game **'Huggy Bear'** with younger children, very familiar or uninhibited groups and ask them to hug each other. Otherwise you can call it **'Clumps'** and give people the choice of a linked-up hug or 'safe' contact by touching fingers.

Why do we like it?

- You can play it at the beginning of a session and refer back to it when you want to split into groups later. You can be creative with your choice of categories.
- Groups establish their own acceptable levels of contact and people find they have things in common with those who may not be their friends.

© Dynamix 2002

4 UP

A problem-solving game to promote concentration and awareness of others.

- 10 - 40 people
- Time: 5 - 10 minutes

How does it work?

The group sits in a circle. You tell them that you are taking them to a strange planet with a very freaky atmosphere. There is no point speaking as the sound will not travel and gravity is such that only four people can stand up at any one time. It is also impossible to remain standing for more than ten seconds. You then challenge the group to go to this planet – you push the imaginary 'start' button and see if they can keep four people standing all the time. If you want to stop the game push the 'button' again to return to earth.

Why do we like it?

- It is a team problem-solving game which groups rarely solve straight away - it is often surprising to groups how difficult it is to play 4 Up.
- You can let them try several ways to keep '4 up' until they find a system that works.
- It works in a classroom setting as well as in a circle.
- You can only really play this once with a group.

I SIT ON THE GRASS

A fairly calm wake-up game using names.

- 15 - 30 people
- Time: 5 - 10 minutes

How does it work?

Everyone sits in a circle, preferably on chairs with one chair left empty. When the game starts the two people on either side of the empty chair attempt to sit on it. The person whose buttocks 'win' the seat shouts "I sit". The person who was sitting next to them moves into their vacated seat and shouts "On the grass". The next person along moves into their vacated seat and says "Next to my friend...Alison". Alison (or whoever they choose) must then leave her seat in the circle and run to sit by her 'friend'. Now Alison's original seat is free so the two people who were either side of her compete for the seat and so the game continues.

© Dynamix 2002

Why do we like it?

·   It can be fast-moving without lots of people running around.
·   People refer to each other as 'friends' – don't underestimate the power of language!
·   "I sit!" can sound a bit rude if you're not careful!

WOULD YOU LIKE NEW NEIGHBOURS?

A circle game to get people moving around.

⬤ 10 - 40 people

⬤ Time: 5 - 10 minutes

How does it work?

Everyone sits in a circle. The facilitator approaches one person and asks them "Would you like new neighbours?" They can answer "yes" or "no". If they say "no" you ask someone else. If they say "yes" then you ask, "who would you like?" They can either say the names of two people in the circle, who must then swap places with the two people on either side, or they can say "anybody", at which point everyone swaps places.

Why do we like it?

·   It encourages people to listen and to move!
·   It is usually funny.
·   The person asking the questions can remain the same or they can take an empty seat when people are moving so that whoever is left without a seat becomes the new caller.

© Dynamix 2002

PART 4
COOKING WITH DYNAMIX: THINGS TO HELP YOU

Introducing the Menus

We have now shared with you our thoughts and ideas about effective participation and provided you with a toolkit of methods. Once you are aware of the aims of your session, know your group and have the necessary background information, you can put together the triangle of aims, content and methods (see page 11). Don't forget icebreakers, making it work and evaluations. As you will see in the next pages, we really do believe they are crucial to making a successful session.

> Don't say we didn't warn you about the food theme!

> The menus are all sessions that worked well and were given good evaluation by the young people.

The following menus or programmes will provide you with ideas for your own programmes and methods. These are real programmes so they don't all follow the same format nor do they only contain only the activities described in this book. We hope they'll show you that participative methods work with different ages and audiences and in different contexts and settings. They represent various stages in different projects' lives: some are for initiating consultation, some for planning and others for evaluation. We are hoping you'll use, adapt and abuse these methods for different fields and different circumstances. Just remember to…

- be flexible
- be enthused
- have lost of ideas ready
- be uninhibited

and

- **HAVE FUN!**

Good luck with your consultations and planning and we hope you've found the book a useful, and enjoyable read.

A:

LAMBETH YOUNG PEOPLE'S PARLIAMENT

Numbers & Age ranges   80 young people, primary & secondary

Consultation with young people and teachers about current local issues in their schools as part of local education authority work on behaviour.

Aims
- To consult young people about acceptable/unacceptable behaviour
- To look at the role of pupils/staff/carers
- To look at supporting vulnerable young people, including those with mental health problems, those who are bullied and Looked After Children
- To look at the effectiveness of exclusion
- To allow young people to mix and share experiences
- To be enjoyable as well as informative

Methodology
- To be participatory
- To have opening and closing activity with all young people mixed together
- To have workshops with mixed schools but separate ages (secondary and primary)
- Some opportunity for schools groups to reflect on taking it back

Content

9.00   Arrivals, welcome, names on sticky labels, activity to start Tables for each school's coats and bags. Lambeth Human Bingo

9.30   Open – welcome speech by LEA

Making it work session
People into smaller groups – name/icebreaker activity
Big Wind Blows; Opinion finders
Diamond Ranking – 'What makes things difficult at school?'
Possibly include: number of friends; other pupils' behaviour; no equipment; playground too small; boring lessons; bullying; unfair punishments; schools falling down; pressure from teachers; pressure from parents

10.45   Break

11.00   Post-its Ideas Storm to develop the issues chosen from
             Diamond Ranking
             Discussion to draw out the underlying issues using:
             Paper Carousel; How How How; Discussion Carousel

12.00   Taking it Forward
             Feedback/evaluation – Evaluation Targets
             Thank you and goodbye

12.30   Lunch and Farewell

B:

LAMBETH PARENTS' JURY

Numbers & Age ranges   30 parents

Consultation with parents/carers about appropriate behaviour, rewards and sanctions – also part of LEA's work on behaviour.

Aims
As per Menu A.

Methodology
· Participative – allowing people to have their voices heard whilst trying to avoid 'case histories'.

Content

10.00	Welcome speech by LEA; explanation about the event; names; Making it Work and show young people's Making it Work from previous day Opinion Finders activity and compare young people's Opinion Finders
10.30	Cotton Bud Debate – 'How can we promote positive behaviour?' Paper Carousel – 'What do people feel responsible for?' 'What should the LEA do?' 'What are the pupils responsible for?'
11.15	Coffee break
11.30	Hot Seating on Looked After Children Post-its Ideas Storm – 'What is bullying?' Discussion Carousel – 'What causes bullying?' How How How – 'How can we stop bullying?'
12.30	Review Taking it Forward (with sign-up board for what they will do to make a difference) Evaluation Targets Thank you from someone important Goodbye

CHILDREN MATTER PROJECT
– SWANSEA PRIMARY SCHOOLS

Numbers & Age ranges   5-11 year olds, 3 primary schools
(approximately 30 from each year)

Consultation on behalf of Barnardo's around improving schools.

Aims
- To be an inclusive process allowing pupils and staff in school the opportunity to get involved
- To make people feel valued and 'own' the process
- To help children take part in making school rules work
- To offer a range of methodology to school staff

Content
- What do young people think about their school?
- What constitutes good and bad behaviour?
- What makes young people happy/sad in school?
- What rewards are currently available and what else could be made available?
- What sanctions are currently available and what else could be made available?
- Who is responsible for different jobs in the school?

Programme
- Hello, welcome, aims, making it work, anonymity, overall picture, name badges
- Icebreaker – Wind Blows – issues
  Do too much work?; brothers/sisters in school?; how you get to school?; seen someone crying?; know children in your class who are happy/sad?; who likes playtime?; who likes ice cream?; seen a fight in your school?

Opinion finders – see Value Continuum adaptation
I am happy in this school; the teachers are friendly in this school; the children are friendly in this school; school is fun; there are lots of different things to do in school; the playground makes me sad; my classroom is horrible

Rights & Responsibilities
- Split into groups with staff aid to collect ideas for next two exercises
- What makes you happy/safe? Post-its
- What makes you sad/unsafe? Post-its
- Follow this up with a talk on responsibilities – who is going to make it better, who cares - could use Wind Blows or Value Continuum

Sanctions
- Generate a list of bad behaviours shown in school – Ideas Avalanche
- Upper school – Value Continuum on sanctions
- Lower school – What happens if...discussion

Rewards
- Diamond Ranking (upper primary)
- Yes/No/Don't know Value Continuum (lower primary)

What happens next? Whole school parliament – inter-school parliament
What do we want them to do? Talk to other classes

Evaluation from Young People
Targets

D:

TOWNHILL YOUTH CONFERENCE PLANNING WEEKEND

Residential weekend with young people and their youth workers to prepare for conference for their peers.

Friday   Aims; Making it work; Chart of Responsibilities

Saturday
10.00   Welcome; aims; Making it Work; timetable; give out folders

10.05   Ice breakers – Human Bingo; Archipelago; Wind Blows;
           Huggy Bear

10.30   Paper Carousel   What makes a good conference?
                             Why have a conference? Who is it for?
           Feedback, Break

11.15   Game
           What's it all about – Post-its/Diamond Ranking – groups of
           three workshops – feedback – overall decision of five
           workshops and Dot Voting

Games and methodologies/team building – need to generate an action
list and note it on the chart of responsibilities

Walk through 10 methodologies we can use, also 5 new methodologies
on workshop content – Cotton Bud Debate; Value Continuum; Hot
Seating; Discussion Carousel; Opinion Finders

12.30   Lunch

1.30   Who's doing what workshops – in groups

The rest of the weekend was spent on teambuilding activities and
refining ideas for the workshops ending on Sunday lunchtime with
'What What What still needs to be done?'

E:

CHILDREN'S COMMISSIONER
INTERVIEW PROCESS EVALUATION

Numbers & Age ranges   16 young people (12 – 19 year olds)

Commissioned by National Assembly for Wales to run an independent evaluation by young people involved in the recruitment and selection process for the Children's Commissioner for Wales.

2pm – 4.15pm:

· Hello, Aims and Introduction

· Dynamix on the Hot Seat and What do you want from today?

· Wind Blows

· Opinion Finders

· Value Continuums – venue, accommodation, food etc

· Paper Carousel in three groups – with Cotton Buds?

   Strengths and weaknesses of: Choosing the young people to be involved; being consulted on key issues; team building and breaking the ice with the group; planning day; interview day; feedback since

· Anonymous feedback in a hat and Graffiti Wall (See Arty Mural)

· Discussion Carousel – 'What else could have made it better?'

· Presentation preparation
   Freeze Frame sketches – wishes for the future?
   Best and worst moments

· Feedback and tea

F:

METROPOLITAN POLICE

Numbers & Age ranges   20-30 young people (11-20 year olds)
(approximately 30 from each year)

Establishing a police liaison committee, improving communication with young people and creating ideas on how to build relationships with young people.

- Introduction of ourselves
- Aims of the consultation and the limitations – we are not black and we are not from Hackney
- Our roles
- What the report could do, where it is going and the weight behind the initiative
- Icebreaker – Wind Blows
- Information gatherer – Opinion Finders:

People should be proud to say they live in Hackney; society is more violent now than it was ten years ago; lack of facilities for young people is the biggest problem in Hackney; everyone suffers from crime; the police treat all young people the same

The police treat all young people with respect; there are too many police on the streets; the police don't listen to young people; police can work in partnership with the community; employment is the biggest issue facing young people; a youth forum is pointless; police need to recruit more people from minority groups.

• Discussion	Outcomes of above activities
• Discussion Carousel	What are the three biggest issues about the police in Hackney and why? A police/young people forum will never work as only one side has power
• Diamond Ranking	What would improve police/community relations? What things should the police concentrate on?
• Ideas Avalanche	What could a police liaison committee do?
• Value Continuum	on whether it would work or not
• Evaluation by form	

6:

RED CROSS CONSULTATION FOR YOUNG PEOPLE

Numbers & Age ranges   approximately 15 young people
(8-13 year olds)

General consultation on the future of Red Cross Youth with groups of young members in six locations across the UK.

10.30	Introduction Hot Seating - Who are we and Who are you? Why we're here What's going to happen?
10.40	Needs for the day Making it work/timetable Aims – not detailed programme
10.45	Icebreaker Games Wind Blows Human Bingo
11.00	Arty Mural – what happens to young people in different parts of the world? Global awareness
12.00	Body in a box – Young people's rights
12.30	Lunch
1.30	Parachute games – adults and young people How children help other children Paper Carousel (Babies/Adults/children)
2.00	What other groups help young people? Ideas Avalanche How are young people's needs met?
2.45	Dreams for Red Cross future Freeze Frame (use digital camera) Speech Balloons/captions
3.15	Presentation
3.45	Evaluation Targets End game – Applaudion Chair

H:

TEC CREATIVE JOBSEARCH TRAINING

Numbers & Age ranges   10 workers

Getting TEC (Training and Enterprise Council) employees who work with young people to devise more creative methods for doing job searches with them.

9.30	Human Bingo & labels
9.45	Who are we & what do we do? Hot Seating
10.00	Wind Blows – Who are you?
10.10	Onion diagram (OHP)
10.20	What we planned & what you want – agenda Amendments – Post-its Ideas Storm
10.40	Making it work
10.50	Break
11.00	Brain theory
11.20	Communication games
12.15	How How How – teaching better interview techniques
1.00	Lunch
1.30	Interview – Jigsaw and Fishbowl
2.15	Self-esteem – Reporters, Stars, Alphabet of positives
3.00	Job search – Cotton Bud Debate and Blind Date
3.30	End games, evaluation techniques (Letter to Yourself)

1:

SCHOOLS COUNCILS – PUPIL'S DAY

Numbers & Age ranges   20-30 young people (6-16 year olds), Primary or secondary, 2 from each class

Five hour day

Working with a group of pupils to develop ideas around establishing school councils (undertaken in various locations).

Aims

· Explore issues
· Look at parameters/power
· Skill up
· Look at self-esteem
· Pitch to senior management team of school

Content

· Hello/Aims/Content/making it work
· Icebreakers – Wind Blows/Opinion Finders
· What is a school council? – definition
· What could it do? – Post-its Ideas Storm, exploring legal, council and school - blocks
· What would be signs of success? – Discussion Carousel
· How big/How often? – Value Continuums
· Teachers – in or out? – Cotton Bud debate
· What would it need? – Diamond Ranking
· Stop and think – methods we have used and could you use them as part of your school council?
· Issues -   Democratic elections
                    Rep. Reps
                    Making real changes
                    Letting everyone know – all Paper Carousel
· Evaluation – Stones in a Pond

J:

BRISTOL YOUNG CARERS CONSULTATION

Numbers & Age ranges   12-15 young carers (8-16 year olds),

The first part of a two part process: the work and ideas generated were taken forward as an action plan to other agencies, some of whom were there on the day.

Aims
- To set up a young carers' voice
- Get your voice heard – what do young carers get/want from social services/education/health?
- Support and produce a work plan
- Review the scheme – what they like/don't like, what is useful/not

Programme
- Introduction; Making it Work; Icebreaker
- The Wind Blows/Opinion Finders – information gathering game
- Value Continuum on project – how long have you been involved/how helpful has it been/are you listened to?
- Post-its Ideas Storm on good/bad things about the project/services from other agencies
- Hot Air Balloon to look at setting up a forum:
  What resources do you need?; what/who would help it to work?; what/who would hold it back?
- Paper Carousel on other agencies and what you want from them
- How How How – action plan to take forward to agencies
- What next for young carers present
- Evaluation Targets (voice heard/had fun/change?)

Potential Games
- Getting to know each other – Zombies, Ball Pass
- Team building/trust games – Knots/Counting to Ten/Points of Contact
- Moving about games – Caterpillar/Do you like your neighbour?
- Parachute games

Opinion Finders - statements to explore
Being a young carer is the most important thing in my life; young carers are very grown up for their age; young carers should get a wage; young carers have no time to go out and have fun; young carers are able to concentrate and do well at school; young carers are given a range of support and services; social workers understand the needs of young carers

Resources
Tool box of all the useful things; flip chart paper and stand; Parachute; Opinion finders sheets; A3 Consultation Balloons; print roll for How How How

K:

CONSULTATION DAY WITH DISABLED YOUNG PEOPLE AND THE NATIONAL ASSEMBLY FOR WALES

Numbers & Age ranges   30 young people (14-18 year olds),

Consultation days to inform and devise a national conference for young disabled people on behalf of the National Assembly for Wales.

Programme
- Making it Work
- Introduce your clothes – secret desires
- The Wind blows
- Diagram illustrating the structure of the Assembly
- Hot Seating   -   Civil Servant
                -   Assembly Member
                -   Senior Assembly Member
- Body in a Box – young human being, a person of your age
- Thing about rights, needs and wants, using a holiday for example
- Impairment cards (extension of Body in a Box) such as
    hidden impairments; challenging Behaviour; communication
    impairments; wheelchair user; mental health system survivor;
    learning difficulties
- Cartwheel – Post-its Ideas Storm, but adapted to be more visual –
  i.e. spokes on a cartwheel are issues such as: Transport, education,
  housing, benefits, social life, relationships, employment, medical, fun
  and empty spokes
- Hot issues (adaptation of Value Continuum - a thermometer on the
  floor with a fire engine at one end and a polar bear at the other!)
  Place issues – Self, friends, wider group – on a temperature line
- Big Ears – choose issues & prioritise – visualise Rhodri Morgan's ear
  and what you want to ask him
- Choose spokespeople – Cotton Bud Debate on how to choose people
- Who – Set ballot paper on day – phone, email, fax the results of the
  ballot
- End – Whooh! Rating

L:

DEVISING YOUNG PEOPLE'S CELEBRATION DAY, WARRINGTON

Working with a planning group of young people to put together a day for 100 other young people to celebrate ten years of the UN Convention on the Rights of the Child.

- Welcome

- Making it Work

- Housekeeping

- Aims of the Day

- Hot Seating – What is Dynamix?

- Welcoming techniques: Human Treasure Hunt; Big Wind Blows; Opinion Finders; Reporters

- Post-its Ideas Storm for ideal day

- Ideas Avalanche to create a Menu

- Wishes and Worries (Hopes and Fears in a Hat) about the day

- Introduction to possibilities for arts and performance workshops from Dynamix

- Dot Voting for workshop content

- How How How for roles for the day

- End games – Web and Sit on My Knees Please!

COMMUNITIES THAT CARE
– RESIDENTIAL WEEKEND

Numbers & Age ranges   8 young people aged 12 – 19
and 8 project workers

Working together to consolidate a vision of ways forward for young people in their community, with the hope that the young people present would form some kind of group.

Aims of the weekend
· Teambuilding
· To be inspiring
· Looking at 'vision' and starting to make it real
· To work out next steps
· To have fun

Friday night
· Arrive; find beds; making it work; food; chill out!

Saturday
Team building, looking at what 'vision' is, fun, energetic
· Aims, reminder of making it work
· The Wind blows; Reporters; Jigsaw; team challenge – newspaper, tape and eggs
· BREAK
· Similarities and differences; Murals (Arty Mural) –
dream community/nightmare community (World's Worst);
yellow post-its – stick on things that already exist in dream picture;
pink post-its – things that are definitely possible; project workers
chat about awareness of where resources come from (keeping it
real); Knots game; Wishes and worries (Hopes and Fears in a Hat)
· LUNCH
· Game – I sit on the grass; feedback of wishes and worries;
game – Bat and moth; Stars; Win win; Communication cards
· BREAK
· Parachute and circus skills on the beach; drawing today together
and we're great!

Sunday

Bringing the vision to life

- Recap making it work; Archipelago – names, number of hours slept, month born; Value Continuums; Shield – themselves, big one about Bonymaen (young people, adults, non-residents, council, dogs and cats etc.)
- BREAK
- Breaking down barriers – Cotton Bud Debate or Talking Stick; Hot Seat youth forums (anyone can ask questions or answer); How How How can we carry on with what we've started?
- LUNCH
- Sustaining improvement – Hot Air Balloon; what happens next? – name your group (Ideas Avalanche followed by Dot Voting) and set up first meeting; post-its commitments; evaluation – Target and Graffiti Walls and Letter to Yourself; Applaudion Chair/pats on the back etc.

BARNARDO'S CHILDREN'S FUND BRISTOL
SESSION 1 of 2 (2 hours)

Consultation with primary school children (including reception) on services they use, are aware of and would like to have. Issues to include education, crime, health, leisure and participation.

- Distribution of name labels; introduction of adults
- Explain aims of session and show the diagram of the process so that the young people can see where they fit in. Be clear about what you can and can't do with their ideas
- Making it Work (Ideas Avalanche)
- Icebreaker Activities
  The Wind Blows (include pertinent questions); Clumps (to identify similarities and differences)
- Value Continuum (or a version of it)
  Yes, No, Sometimes (or Don't Know) asking a range of questions
  e.g. Do you like living in this area?; Do you like getting up
  in the morning?
  A facilitator at each point (yes, no, don't know) asks the
  children why they have chosen that response and writes
  down the ideas expressed
- Rights Body
  Draw around a child on a large piece of paper (wallpaper, print rolls), and ask "What do children need?". Emphasis on needs and rights not wants and desires. Once you have gathered some ideas, likely to be around food, clothes, family etc, ask questions beyond their likely personal experience (see questions list)
- BREAK
- Health Issues
  Potential activity – Paper Carousel. Three questions: i. What does a healthy person eat? ii. What does a healthy person look like? iii. What does a healthy person like to do?
- World's Worst
  Describe the world's worst area to live in. Choice of activities
  (split into two groups): i. individual pictures or an Arty Mural (felt tips, pencils etc) ii. song making. Groups feedback to each other
  In light of exploring the World's Worst, discuss what makes a good place to live and what would make your area a better place to live in. Methodology? Small groups discuss and feedback OR Cotton Bud Debate OR Talking Stick.
- Self-esteem game - Applaudion Chair

FURTHER READING AND RESOURCES

They don't just write books they read them too......

.... here are some they like....

The following publications provide more background, ideas and methodology around working with children and young people and promoting participation.

General

Madden, S. (2001) **Re:action consultation toolkit: a practical toolkit for consulting with children and young people on policy issues**, Save the Children, Scotland

Youth Council for Northern Ireland (2001) **Seen and Heard? Consulting and involving young people within the public sector**, YCNI, Northern Ireland

Treseder, P. (1997) **Empowering children and young people: Training manual**, Save the Children, London. ISBN 1 899120 47 5

Crowley and Treseder (2001) **Taking the Initiative: Promoting young people's involvement in local decision making**, (Wales) Carnegie Young People Initiative

Tolley, E. Girma, M., Stanton-Wharmby, A. Spate, A. and Milburn, J. (1998) **Young Opinions: Great Ideas**, National Children's Bureau, London

National Youth Agency (2001) **Speaking Out: Young people, consultation and decision making**, NYA, Leicester, Video

Fajerman, L. and Treseder, P. (2000) **Children are Service Users Too : A guide to consulting with children and young people**, Save the Children. ISBN 1 84187 051 X

Hart, R. (1992) **Children's Participation: From tokenism to citizenship**, UNICEF

Eric Jensen, **The Learning Brain**, Turning Point Publishing ISBN 0 9637832 2 X

Carolyn Hamilton. **Working with Young People: Legal responsibility and liability**, 5th Edition, The Children's Legal Centre

Local Government

Willow, C. (1997) **Hear! Hear!: Promoting children and young people's democratic participation in local government**, Local Government Information Unit, London

Wade, H. Lawton, A. and Stevenson, M. (2001) **Hear by right: Setting standards for the active involvement of young people in democracy**, Local Government Association/ National Youth Agency, London and Leicester

White, P. (2001) **Local and Vocal: Promoting young people's involvement in local decision making – an overview and planning guide**, Save the Children and National Youth Agency

Association of Metropolitan Authorities and Children's Rights Office. **Checklist for Children: Local authorities and the United Nations Convention on the Rights of the Child**

Health

Cohen, J. and Emanuel, J. (1998) **Positive Participation, Consulting with Children and Young People in Health-related Work: A planning and training resource**, Health Education Authority, London

McNeish, D. (1999) **From Rhetoric to Reality: Participatory approaches to health promotion with young people**, Health Education authority

Mental Health

Laws, S. (1998) **Hear Me! Consulting with young people on mental health services**, Mental Health Foundation, London

Waitt, C. (1998) **Reaching out: Consultation with 'hard to reach' users of mental health services**, Barnardos

Disability

Griffiths, J., Cunningham, G. and Dick, S. (1999) **Onwards and Upwards, Involving Disabled Children and Young People in Decision Making: A training manual for professionals**, Children in Scotland

Education

Greenaway, M. (comp.) (1999) **Give us a Choice…Give us a Voice: Children and young people's consultation in the city and county of Swansea**, City and County of Swansea, Swansea

Sutton, F. et al.(1999) **The School Council: A children's guide**. Save the Children (Midlands Development Team)

Paul Ginnis, **The Teacher's Toolkit**, Crown House Publishing. ISBN 189983676 4

Play and Leisure

Article 31 action consultancy scheme: Children as consultants to arts, media and leisure service providers, Playtrain, 31 Farm Road. Sparkbrook Birmingham B11 1LS 0121 766 8446 www.playtrn.demon.co.uk

The children's play information service – CPIS – specialist information resource providing information on aspects of children's play. Based at National Children's Bureau, 8 Wakely Street, London, 0207 843 6303. CPIS@ncb.org.uk

Dynamix: **Serious Fun - Games for 4-9 Year Olds** (Can Do Series, Thomson Learning). ISBN 1 86152 837 X

Dynamix: **Serious Fun - Games for 10-14 Year Olds** (Can Do Series, Thomson Learning). ISBN 1 86152 839 6

Meynell. **Meynell Games On…Parachute play**, ISBN 1 898068 00 3

Our parachute suppliers are **Seamstress Ltd**, 23 Banbury Road, Byfield, Northants, NN11 6XT 01327 263933

Environment

Adams, E. and Ingham, S. (1998) **Changing Places: Children's participation in environmental planning**, The Children's Society, London

Community

Johnson, V., Ivan-Smith, E., Gordon G., Pridmore, P. and Scott, P. (Eds) **Stepping Forward: Children and young people's participation in the development process**, International Technology Publications, London

Save the Children (1997) **All together now: Community participation for children and young people**, Save the Children, London.

Fitzpatrick, S., Hastings, A., and Kintrea, K. (1998) **Including Young People in Urban Regeneration: A lot to learn?** The Policy Press, London

Matthews, H., **Children and Community Regeneration: Creating better neighbourhoods**, Save the Children, London.

Social Services/looked after children and young people

CROA and DoH (2000) **Total Respect: Training pack**, CROA, London www.croa.org.uk

Thomas, N. and O'Kane, C. (1997) **Children and Decision Making: Toolkit**, Children in Wales, Cardiff

Who Cares? Trust (1999) **Remember My Messages**, Who Cares? Trust, London www.wct.org.uk

Young Children

Clark, A. and Moss, P. (2001) **Listening to Young Children: The mosaic approach**, National Children's Bureau, London

Miller, J. (1997) **Never too Young: How young children can take responsibility and make decisions**, Save the Children/ National Early Years Network

Fajerman, L. Jarrett, M. Sutton, F. (2000) **Children as Partners in Planning**, Save the Children.

Miller, J. (1999) **A Journey of Discovery: Children's creative participation in planning**, Save the Children, ISBN 1 870985 34 6

Rural Children and Young People

Williams, J. (2000) **Think Country Child! The councillors guide to planning services for children and young people in rural areas**, NCVCCO, CA, LGA, London.

INDEX: ACTIVITIES

INDEX: MENUS

SAMPLES

Human Bingo sheet example – youth forum

Human Bingo pro forma

Opinion Finders pro forma

Hot Air Balloon example

Hot Air Balloon pro forma

Lifeline pro forma

Jigsaw example

YOUTH FORUM BINGO

1 person who has had their photo in a newspaper	2 people with a Saturday job	2 people who have travelled more than five miles to be here	3 people who have not got mobile phones
1 person involved in a school council	1 person who has never smoked/tried a cigarette	1 person who is a parent	2 people who have caught a bus today
3 people who believe animals have rights	2 people who have been asked their opinions in town	2 people who have pretended to be ill to get off school or work	2 people who hate S Club 7
1 person who has never owned any Marks & Spencers underwear	2 people who are not wearing trainers	1 person who likes speaking in public	1 person who thinks that adults are fair to young people

HUMAN BINGO

OPINION FINDERS

STATEMENT

	Tally	Totals
Agree Strongly		
Agree		
No Opinion		
Disagree		
Disagree Strongly		

Comments

HOT AIR BALLOON

OUR ENTHUSIASM!

People Moving On

Fading Commitment

Regular meetings

Move venue – same day & time

Big Target & small ones – define aims & achievement

Keep people interested

Fun

Lack of confidence in Council & Adults

OUR YOUTH FORUM

Identity

Fundraising

Check out our views with other young people

Advertising

Training

People interested in improving youth facilities

Volunteers, Councillors, Schools, Police (for support)

Young people with adults to support them (not take over)

People with money/ who can fill in forms

IDZ4U

Being too busy to commit

Funding

Lack of ideas

Nobody involved

People not having a say

Same people all the time

Just talking – No action

Lack of confidence

HOT AIR BALLOON

MY LIFELINE

by ....

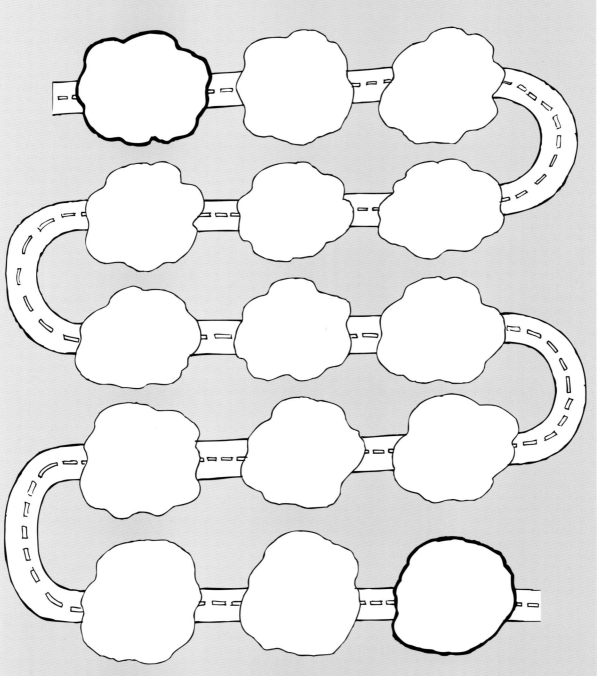

Serious Fun
Serious Fun
Serious Fun
Serious Fun

JIGSAW

CONGRATULATIONS!

We hope your group is complete.
Please check that you
know everyone's names.

You have 5 minutes to complete
the following tasks.
Collect paper and pens from the desk.

****

1. List five skills you need to work in a team.

2. Draw a picture of a brain

3. Label three areas of the brain

4. List five things you can do to help your
    brain work

PART 5
MORE ABOUT DYNAMIX

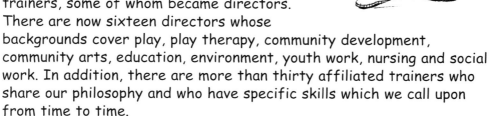

Once upon a time there was Dynamix.... here's a bit about who they are and what they do....

Dynamix is a workers' co-operative which was set up in 1988 in response to the two founding directors' experiences of unimaginative and often ineffective training. Over the following years, Dynamix worked with more and more trainers, some of whom became directors. There are now sixteen directors whose backgrounds cover play, play therapy, community development, community arts, education, environment, youth work, nursing and social work. In addition, there are more than thirty affiliated trainers who share our philosophy and who have specific skills which we call upon from time to time.

Dynamix provides creative and innovative training designed to suit the needs of each individual group, and that means anyone. Our work has ranged from anti-bullying sessions for under fives to inclusive circus skills workshops with the Women's Institute. We also work with service providers (youth workers, teachers), service users (school children, members of the public) or a mixture of both. Buzzwords we over-use include participative, co-operative, inclusive, non-judgemental, developmental, empowerment, creative, innovative and fun.

Dynamix's work in promoting youth participation has spanned the UK and reached further afield. We have worked with a diverse range of organisations including schools, police forces, local authorities, providers of services for looked after children, health authorities, large charities such as Save the Children, Barnardos and the Red Cross, as well as small local organisations. A large proportion of our work takes place in Wales, where we are based, and we are pleased to be working on a series of projects with the National Assembly for Wales including the training of the Youth Policy Unit.

Our work is primarily about training others in using these methods or helping to kick start a consultation process: our role is not to manage individual projects. However, the following examples illustrate the impact that can be made when an input of Dynamix values, methods and enthusiasm is coupled with the energy and commitment of the organisations concerned.

Carol Shephard, Dynamix, July 2002

Five Case Studies

Have a look at these stories about good stuff that has happened to and for young people

Claire O'Kane, a former Dynamix worker, went to work for Butterflies, a non-government organisation project working with street children in India. Claire was able to incorporate some of the participative methods she had been using with Dynamix into her work with these children (around children's rights issues) as well as with street educators working with children. Consultation and priority-setting activities such as Diamond Ranking have enabled children to explore the priority issues they would like to study. These methods have also helped adults to explore what child participation really means to them. Furthermore, through their own Delhi Child Rights Club, child workers from across Delhi used mapping and visual ranking to identify priority problems in their communities. They then took concrete action to raise community awareness and encourage people to act on their priorities. Street educators for the project continue to use some of the methods in their street work and training.

At a time when relations between the police and young people were disintegrating to crisis point, an inspector from the Metropolitan Police approached Dynamix to facilitate a consultation and dialogue with local young people and police officers. Once Dynamix was satisfied that this was a genuine attempt to truly consult and listen to the young people, it agreed to facilitate the process. From a starting point of no positive communication, a Youth Advisory Committee was formed, regular consultations took place, and tensions were greatly relieved. A programme from this consultation appears in the Menu Section (page 125).

The Children's Rights Development Unit was set up to monitor and evaluate the UK government's progress in implementing the United Nations Convention on the Rights of the Child. It contracted Dynamix to facilitate a weekend conference and consultation to explore the possibility of establishing a child-led children's rights organisation. This conference, sponsored by Channel 4 to coincide with the launch of new children's rights based programmes, led directly to the formation of Article 12, one of the first children-led children's rights organisations in the UK. Many of the methods in this book were used at that conference, and continue to be used by the young people at Article 12 events.

Promoting Positive Behaviour is an ongoing project in schools in the Swansea area. Consultation that took place with young people in three secondary schools about behaviour, sanctions and rewards directly informed a behaviour policy and plan which was written by the local authority's Education Committee. There has since been a considerable reduction in the number of permanent exclusions. The impact on the individual schools was such that the programme has been rolled out to nine secondary schools with a plan to include all schools in the area including eventually primary schools.

On behalf of the Welsh Assembly, Dynamix undertook three consultations across Wales with groups of disabled young people (see Menu K, page 131). These led to an event to mark International Day of Disabled People which included a special question time in the Assembly Chamber with the young people, Rhodri Morgan, the First Minister and Edwina Hart, Minister for Finance, Local Government and Communities and Chair of the Equal Opportunities Committee.

On 10 January 2002 a motion was passed by the Assembly which stated that it:

1. Welcomes the event held on 3 December 2001 to mark the International Day of Disabled People and notes the success of the event and the questions put forward by the young people during the question time session.

2. Recognises the important role that young people, and specifically young disabled people, have in developing Assembly policy.

3. Notes that the policy of inclusion will be pursued across Cabinet portfolios and on a systematic basis.

4. Accepts the validity of the social model of disability and acknowledges the need to mainstream this principle in the policies of the National Assembly.

In a letter from the National Assembly the young people were told: "This Motion came about directly through your hard work and the positive image each of you displayed at the event. You asked that the Assembly listen and they have listened."